Choosing
Sides

Jean Paré

www.companyscoming.com
visit our website

Front Cover

1. Grilled Curry Potatoes, page 68
2. Snow Pea Jicama Stir-Fry, page 129
3. Tangy Carrots, page 134

Props courtesy of: Mikasa
Home Store

Back Cover

1. Tomato Pesto Biscotti, page 25
2. Tabbouleh, page 41
3. Sweet Peppers And Almonds, page 128

Props courtesy of: Casa Bugatti
Stokes

We gratefully acknowledge the following suppliers for their generous support of our Test and Photography Kitchens:

Broil King Barbecues   *Hamilton Beach® Canada*   *Proctor Silex® Canada*
Corelle®   *Lagostina®*   *Tupperware®*

Choosing Sides

First Printing May 2008

Library and Archives Canada Cataloguing in Publication
Paré, Jean, date-
Choosing sides /Jean Paré.
(Original series)
Includes index.
ISBN 978-1-897069-51-6
1. Side dishes (Cookery) I. Title. II. Series: Paré, Jean, date-. Original series.
TX740.P37 2008   641.8'1   C2007-905155-3

Published by
Company's Coming Publishing Limited
2311 – 96 Street
Edmonton, Alberta, Canada T6N 1G3
Tel: 780-450-6223   Fax: 780-450-1857
www.companyscoming.com

We acknowledge the financial support of the Government of Canada through the Book Publishing Industry Development Program (BPIDP) for our publishing activities.

Printed in China

Need more recipes?

Six *"sneak preview"* recipes are featured online **with every new book released**.

Visit us at
www.companyscoming.com

Company's Coming Cookbooks

Original Series

- Softcover, 160 pages
- 6" x 9" (15 cm x 23 cm) format
- Lay-flat plastic comb binding
- Full-colour photos
- Nutrition information

Quick & easy recipes! Everyday ingredients!

Lifestyle Series

- Softcover, 160 pages
- 8" x 10" (20 cm x 25 cm) format
- Paperback
- Full-colour photos
- Nutrition information

Most Loved Recipe Collection

- Hardcover, 128 pages
- 8 3/4" x 8 3/4" (22 cm x 22 cm) format
- Durable sewn binding
- Full-colour throughout
- Nutrition information

Special Occasion Series

- Hardcover concealed wiro
- 8 1/2" x 11" (22 cm x 28 cm) format
- Lay-flat binding
- Full-colour throughout
- Nutrition information

See page 157 for more cookbooks.
For a complete listing, visit
www.companyscoming.com

Table of Contents

The Company's Coming Story

Jean Paré (pronounced "jeen PAIR-ee") grew up understanding that the combination of family, friends and home cooking is the best recipe for a good life. From her mother, she learned to appreciate good cooking, while her father praised even her earliest attempts in the kitchen. When Jean left home, she took with her a love of cooking, many family recipes and an intriguing desire to read cookbooks as if they were novels!

"never share a recipe you wouldn't use yourself"

In 1963, when her four children had all reached school age, Jean volunteered to cater the 50th Anniversary of the Vermilion School of Agriculture, now Lakeland College, in Alberta, Canada. Working out of her home, Jean prepared a dinner for more than 1,000 people, which launched a flourishing catering operation that continued for over 18 years. During that time, she had countless opportunities to test new ideas with immediate feedback—resulting in empty plates and contented customers! Whether preparing cocktail sandwiches for a house party or serving a hot meal for 1,500 people, Jean Paré earned a reputation for good food, courteous service and reasonable prices.

As requests for her recipes mounted, Jean was often asked the question, "Why don't you write a cookbook?" Jean responded by teaming up with her son, Grant Lovig, in the fall of 1980 to form Company's Coming Publishing Limited. The publication of *150 Delicious Squares* on April 14, 1981 marked the debut of what would soon become one of the world's most popular cookbook series.

The company has grown since those early days when Jean worked from a spare bedroom in her home. Today, she continues to write recipes while working closely with the staff of the Recipe Factory, as the Company's Coming test kitchen is affectionately known. There she fills the role of mentor, assisting with the development of recipes people most want to use for everyday cooking and easy entertaining. Every Company's Coming recipe is *kitchen-tested* before it's approved for publication.

Jean's daughter, Gail Lovig, is responsible for marketing and distribution, leading a team that includes sales personnel located in major cities across Canada. In addition, Company's Coming cookbooks are published and distributed under licence in the United States, Australia and other world markets. Bestsellers many times over in English, Company's Coming cookbooks have also been published in French and Spanish.

Familiar and trusted in home kitchens around the world, Company's Coming cookbooks are offered in a variety of formats. Highly regarded as kitchen workbooks, the softcover Original Series, with its lay-flat plastic comb binding, is still a favourite among readers.

Jean Paré's approach to cooking has always called for *quick and easy recipes* using *everyday ingredients.* That view has served her well. The recipient of many awards, including the Queen Elizabeth Golden Jubilee medal, Jean was appointed a Member of the Order of Canada, her country's highest lifetime achievement honour.

Jean continues to gain new supporters by adhering to what she calls The Golden Rule of Cooking: *"Never share a recipe you wouldn't use yourself."* It's an approach that works— *millions of times over!*

6

Foreword

Side dishes often seem to be the afterthought of our meal planning—as long as we have our main dish set the rest will come easy, right? Wrong! You might be able to put an awe-inspiring entree on the table night after night, but your meals will soon seem lacklustre if they are always accompanied by the same old mashed potatoes and frozen peas.

Choosing Sides is our solution to this dreadful dinner dilemma. No matter what your main dish is, you'll be able to accompany it with flair! We've hit all the bases with beans, lentils, breads, pasta, potatoes, rice, grains and vegetables. So, whatever you're craving, we've got you covered—from old favourites like Simple Cheddar Scalloped Potatoes, page 63, to adventurous new flavours like Curried Okra And Tomato, page 124. We've even included a special Sauces & Condiments chapter so you can whip up your own extra-special versions of dinner-table staples like relish, ketchup and mustard.

When we developed this book, we took a logical approach to making meals. We knew that you wouldn't want to spend twice as much time preparing and cooking your sides as you did your main dish, so we developed recipes that use easy methods

but still yield great results in a reasonable amount of time.

And to make meal planning trouble-free, we've devised a Sides Guide that gives you easy rules to follow when choosing a side. To make it even simpler, if we felt a particular side was especially well-suited to a particular main, we mentioned it in the recipe introduction. Why guess when we have the information for you?

So, whether you're whipping up frozen fish sticks or your world-famous prime rib, we can help you choose a side that will make any meal truly magnificent!

Jean Paré

Nutrition Information Guidelines

Each recipe is analyzed using the most current version of the Canadian Nutrient File from Health Canada, which is based on the United States Department of Agriculture (USDA) Nutrient Database.

- If more than one ingredient is listed (such as "butter or hard margarine"), or if a range is given (1 – 2 tsp., 5 – 10 mL), only the first ingredient or first amount is analyzed.

- For meat, poultry and fish, the serving size per person is based on the recommended 4 oz. (113 g) uncooked weight (without bone), which is 2 – 3 oz. (57 – 85 g) cooked weight (without bone)—approximately the size of a deck of playing cards.

- Milk used is 1% M.F. (milk fat), unless otherwise stated.

- Cooking oil used is canola oil, unless otherwise stated.

- Ingredients indicating "sprinkle," "optional," or "for garnish" are not included in the nutrition information.

- The fat in recipes and combination foods can vary greatly depending on the sources and types of fats used in each specific ingredient. For these reasons, the amount of saturated, monounsaturated and polyunsaturated fats may not add up to the total fat content.

Vera C. Mazurak, Ph.D.
Nutritionist

The Sides Guide

Choosing the perfect sides

When deciding what side to serve with your masterpiece entree, there are six easy rules of thumb for getting the biggest gastronomical bang for your buck:

Choose complementary tastes. We know you're aware that some things just don't go well together. You'd never serve a side of pickled beets with a bowl of French onion soup, but what about having too much of a good thing? You certainly wouldn't want to serve a cheesy pasta with a side of cauliflower in cheese sauce accompanied by cheese toast. You want to serve sides that complement your entree without battling for dominance. If you're serving something salty, like ham, you may want to choose a sweet side to balance out the flavours. If you're serving a spicy enchilada, a cool and refreshing side will offer your guests a respite from the spicy heat. And if you're serving an entree with a flavourful sauce or gravy, you may want to serve a more neutral side, like rice, that can soak up that sauce rather than compete with it.

Coordinate your colours. Nothing's more drab than a plate full of white food. Choosing the right side gives you a chance to add some appetizing colour. Consider adding a vibrant bean salad to a grilled chicken breast or a little bundle of blanched asparagus to your best steak recipe. Nothing perks up a plate, not to mention an appetite, like a flamboyant flash of colour.

Opt for a variety of textures. There's a reason a nice slice of focaccia bread is so satisfying with soup—you get a variety of textures. Mashed potatoes, roast beef and tender-crisp veggies? Again, you get a nice range of textures. So if your entree's softer, consider adding a crunchy coleslaw side. And if your main attraction is a steak you can really sink your teeth into, consider serving a side of creamy mashed potatoes.

Choose a complementary cooking method. If you are preparing an entree that takes a lot of time or effort, you may choose to make an easy slow cooker side that you won't need to worry about. Or, if your entree is quick and easy, try pairing it with a side you prepare in the microwave that will be ready in about the same amount of time. If you are using your oven or barbecue for your entree, why not make your side at the same time? Just remember to select a side dish that uses the same oven or barbecue temperature.

Balance your meals. To get all the nutrition you need out of your food, you'll want to make sure that your plate has a proper representation of protein, starches and fruits or veggies.

Be kind to your pocketbook. It's sad but true—when it comes to fruits and vegetables, prices vary radically. Come fall, tomatoes are a bargain, but in spring they become a precious commodity. If a certain crop has a bad year, that's going to be reflected in its ever-escalating price. So be aware of the seasons in which various fruits and veggies are plentiful and, therefore, inexpensive. Let that help guide your dinner options.

Keeping all these rules in mind, there is one very important point you should consider: if you're cooking it, it should be something you enjoy eating. In our minds, the cook's taste buds always come first!

The unusual suspects

Certainly one of the best parts of cooking is trying new ingredients. In Choosing Sides, *we decided to explore some of those "odd" ingredients you see in your supermarket but, perhaps, don't have a clue how to prepare. Listed below is a little bit of background info on these unusual suspects to give you a hand in buying and using them.*

arborio rice (pronounced ar-BOH-ree-oh) ~ Used primarily for risotto, this Italian rice has a very high starch content that enables it to give dishes a creamy texture you wouldn't achieve with regular rice.

black-eyed peas ~ A beige bean with a characteristic black "eye" on its inner curve. Popular in southern United States cuisine, these little legumes actually come from Asia. They can be bought dried or in cans.

bok choy ~ When properly cooked, this vegetable's celery-like stalks remain quite crisp and its dark green, romaine lettuce-like leaves become tender. When buying, look for firm stalks and unblemished leaves. Keep wrapped in paper towel in the crisper.

bulgur ~ Simply wheat kernels that have been steamed, dried and crushed. Nutrition-packed bulgur is often confused with cracked wheat—but bulgur has been parboiled and can be cooked quite quickly or even just soaked prior to eating.

daikon radish (pronounced DI-kon) ~ These large Japanese radishes look like white carrots and have a sweet, fresh, crisp taste. Choose firm, blemish-free daikon, but don't opt for the bigger ones—their texture may be too woody. Store in the fridge in a plastic bag. Peel with a potato peeler.

edamame (pronounced eh-dah-MAH-meh) ~ Young soybeans that are sold in fuzzy green pods (don't worry, you won't be eating the pods!). You can buy them fresh in spring, summer and early fall—though they are also available frozen year-round.

fennel ~ Featuring an onion-like bulb, celery-like stalks and dark, feathery green leaves, fennel has a delicate licorice taste. Look for a white, unblemished bulb and bright green leaves. Store in the fridge, tightly wrapped in plastic.

jicama (pronounced HEE-kah-mah) ~ A bulbous root vegetable that's covered in a papery-thin brown skin that must be removed. Jicama has a sweet, crisp white flesh. Store in the fridge, wrapped in plastic.

kale ~ With a mild cabbage-like taste, kale has frilly green leaves with a blue or purplish tinge. Choose richly-coloured, smaller bunches free of yellowing or limp leaves. Purchase just prior to using and store in the fridge. The tough centre stalks must be removed before using.

kohlrabi (pronounced kohl-RAH-bee) ~ With a large white or purple bulb and green leaves, kohlrabi has a mild turnip flavour. Choose bulbs that are firm and heavy but under three inches (7.6 cm) in diameter. Store in the fridge, tightly wrapped in plastic.

okra ~ These small green pods have a bulky stem and contain a liquid that thickens when cooked. Choose brightly coloured okra approximately four inches (10 cm) long. Store in a plastic bag in the fridge. Available fresh or frozen.

orzo ~ Simply, a quick-cooking, tiny rice-shaped pasta.

plantain (pronounced PLAN-tihn) ~ Though they look like large bananas, plantains require cooking. Use at any stage of ripeness from green to black, remembering that the greener they are, the less sweet they will be. Plantains should be firm, no matter the colour. Ripen at room temperature.

polenta ~ A popular Italian staple, polenta is made of cornmeal and generally has a porridge-like consistency. It is also commonly bought in a firmer form that can be easily sliced and heated.

quinoa (pronounced keen-WAH) ~ Although it contains more protein than any other grain, quinoa is tiny, beige and bead-like, with a very delicate taste. It cooks quickly and has an unusual but pleasant texture. Quinoa must always be rinsed prior to cooking.

rutabaga ~ Often thought of as yellow turnips, rutabagas are large, weighty and have a tough yellowish skin that must be removed. Choose rutabagas that are heavy and have a smooth, firm skin. Store in a plastic bag in the fridge.

soba noodles ~ Available in either thick or thin varieties, soba is a Japanese noodle made from buckwheat.

suey choy ~ Similar in flavour to bok choy, suey choy, also known as Chinese cabbage, is cylindrical and has light green leaves. Keep wrapped in paper towel in the crisper.

swiss chard ~ With thick, crisp stalks and lush green leaves, Swiss chard is most commonly available in the summer. Choose chard with firm stalks and unblemished leaves. Store in the fridge in a plastic bag.

tomatillo (pronounced tohm-ah-TEE-oh) ~ Similar in appearance to a small, green tomato in a papery husk, tomatillos have a slightly sour taste that mellows when cooked. Choose tomatillos with tight husks, which are removed before using. Store in a paper bag in the fridge. Wash well prior to use.

Three-Bean Salad

Good things come in threes—that's why we've added not one, not two, but three kinds of beans to this fresh-tasting salad of veggies and herbs. Perfect for the potluck or the picnic because it's great served at room temperature.

Can of chickpeas (garbanzo beans), rinsed and drained	19 oz.	540 mL
Can of navy beans, rinsed and drained	19 oz.	540 mL
Can of red kidney beans, rinsed and drained	19 oz.	540 mL
Diced celery	1 cup	250 mL
Chopped fresh parsley	1/2 cup	125 mL
Finely chopped red onion	1/2 cup	125 mL
Chopped fresh rosemary	2 tsp.	10 mL
Apple cider vinegar	1/4 cup	60 mL
Granulated sugar	1/4 cup	60 mL
Olive oil	3 tbsp.	50 mL
Salt	1 tsp.	5 mL
Pepper	1/4 tsp.	1 mL

Combine first 7 ingredients in large bowl.

Whisk remaining 5 ingredients in small bowl. Drizzle over bean mixture. Toss. Makes about 8 cups (2 L).

1 cup (250 mL): 446 Calories; 10.0 g Total Fat (4.7 g Mono, 2.3 g Poly, 466 g Sat); 0 mg Cholesterol; 70 g Carbohydrate; 15 g Fibre; 21 g Protein; 466 mg Sodium

Pictured on page 71.

Tuscan Bean Salad

Instant Italian! Just toss together a few pantry staples and you've got a perfect side for roasted chicken, pork or grilled spicy sausages.

Can of mixed beans, rinsed and drained	19 oz.	540 mL
Antipasto	1 cup	250 mL
Finely chopped fennel bulb (white part only)	1/2 cup	125 mL
Italian dressing	2 tbsp.	30 mL

(continued on next page)

Beans & Lentils

Combine all 4 ingredients in large bowl. Makes about 3 cups (750 mL).

1 cup (250 mL): 298 Calories; 11.4 g Total Fat (5.3 g Mono, 3 g Poly, 0.8 g Sat); 10 mg Cholesterol; 40 g Carbohydrate; 10 g Fibre; 13 g Protein; 889 mg Sodium

CAESAR BEAN SALAD: Use the same amount of creamy Caesar dressing instead of Italian dressing.

Tomato Chickpeas

The Middle East's favourite legume, the chickpea, goes on an Italian holiday when it's drenched in an herbed tomato sauce. Serve with pork or chicken.

Can of chickpeas (garbanzo beans), rinsed and drained	19 oz.	540 mL
Can of diced tomatoes (with juice)	14 oz.	398 mL
Chopped celery	1/4 cup	60 mL
Chopped onion	1/4 cup	60 mL
Tomato paste (see Tip, page 101)	1 tbsp.	15 mL
Dried oregano	1/2 tsp.	2 mL
Dried rosemary, crushed	1/4 tsp.	1 mL
Garlic clove, minced (or 1/4 tsp., 1 mL, powder)	1	1
Dried crushed chilies	1/8 tsp.	0.5 mL
Bay leaf	1	1

Combine all 10 ingredients in large saucepan. Bring to a boil. Reduce heat to medium-low. Cook, covered, for about 20 minutes, stirring occasionally, until thickened. Remove and discard bay leaf. Makes about 3 cups (750 mL).

1 cup (250 mL): 692 Calories; 11.0 g Total Fat (2.5 g Mono, 4.9 g Poly, 1.2 g Sat); 0 mg Cholesterol; 118 g Carbohydrate; 19 g Fibre; 36 g Protein; 419 mg Sodium

Paré Pointer
The worst month for the Army is March.

Carib-Beans And Rice

*Hearty mixtures of rice and beans are popular throughout
the Caribbean—and we're sure they'll be popular in your house too!
Our version is tamed down for timid taste buds, but you can substitute
a whole Scotch bonnet pepper for the cayenne if you like things
scorching hot—just remember to remove the pepper before serving.*

Bacon slices, diced	2	2
Chopped onion	1/2 cup	125 mL
Diced red pepper	1/2 cup	125 mL
Garlic clove, minced	1	1
(or 1/4 tsp., 1 mL, powder)		
Can of red kidney beans, rinsed and drained	14 oz.	398 mL
Prepared chicken broth	1 1/4 cups	300 mL
Canned coconut milk	1 cup	250 mL
Dried thyme	1/2 tsp.	2 mL
Ground allspice	1/8 tsp.	0.5 mL
Cayenne pepper, just a pinch		
Long grain white rice	3/4 cup	175 mL
Salt	1/4 tsp.	1 mL
Chopped green onion (optional)	2 tbsp.	30 mL

Cook bacon in large saucepan on medium until crisp. Drain all but 1 tsp.
(5 mL) drippings.

Add next 3 ingredients. Cook for about 5 minutes, stirring occasionally,
until onion is softened.

Add next 6 ingredients. Stir. Bring to a boil.

Add rice and salt. Stir. Reduce heat to medium-low. Simmer, covered,
for about 20 minutes, without stirring, until rice is tender and liquid
is absorbed.

Sprinkle with green onion. Makes about 4 cups (1 L).

*1 cup (250 mL): 414 Calories; 16.4 g Total Fat (1.8 g Mono, 0.6 g Poly, 12.4 g Sat);
5 mg Cholesterol; 55 g Carbohydrate; 10 g Fibre; 13 g Protein; 694 mg Sodium*

Pictured on page 17.

Roasted Chickpea Salad

This unique medley of chunky cauliflower and crunchy pecans, soft chickpeas, and salty feta provides the perfect partner to grilled pork or chicken.

Olive (or cooking) oil	1/4 cup	60 mL
Red wine vinegar	2 tbsp.	30 mL
Lemon juice	1 tbsp.	15 mL
Dried oregano	1/2 tsp.	2 mL
Garlic powder	1/2 tsp.	2 mL
Salt	1/2 tsp.	2 mL
Pepper	1/4 tsp.	1 mL
Cauliflower florets	2 cups	500 mL
Pecan halves	1 cup	250 mL
Can of chickpeas (garbanzo beans), rinsed and drained, blotted dry	19 oz.	540 mL
Crumbled feta cheese	1/3 cup	75 mL

Whisk first 7 ingredients in small bowl.

Put cauliflower and pecans into medium bowl. Add 1/4 cup (60 mL) olive oil mixture. Toss until coated. Spread on greased baking sheet with sides. Bake in 400°F (205°C) oven for about 10 minutes until cauliflower is tender-crisp and pecans are starting to brown.

Add chickpeas. Stir. Bake for about 10 minutes, stirring once, until cauliflower is browned and pecans are toasted. Transfer to serving bowl.

Add cheese and remaining olive oil mixture. Stir. Serve immediately or at room temperature. Makes about 3 1/2 cups (875 mL).

1 cup (250 mL): 966 Calories; 50.1 g Total Fat (26.7 g Mono, 12.2 g Poly, 7.2 g Sat); 13 mg Cholesterol; 102 g Carbohydrate; 20 g Fibre; 36 g Protein; 553 mg Sodium

Pictured on page 17.

Lentil Bulgur Pilaf

*This stylish combo of bulgur, lentils and crisp red pepper is sure to be
the "grain" attraction when paired with a beef, chicken or pork entree.
If you like more spice, increase the amount of dried crushed chilies.*

Finely chopped onion	1 cup	250 mL
Prepared vegetable broth	1 cup	250 mL
Bulgur	1/2 cup	125 mL
Sesame oil (for flavour)	1/2 tsp.	2 mL
Dried crushed chilies	1/4 tsp.	1 mL
Fennel seed	1/4 tsp.	1 mL
Salt	1/4 tsp.	1 mL
Pepper	1/4 tsp.	1 mL
Diced red pepper	2 cups	500 mL
Can of lentils, rinsed and drained	19 oz.	540 mL

Combine first 8 ingredients in medium microwave-safe bowl. Microwave,
covered, on high (100%) for 10 minutes.

Add red pepper and lentils. Stir. Microwave, covered, on high (100%)
for 2 to 4 minutes until red pepper is tender-crisp. Makes about
5 1/2 cups (1.4 L).

*1 cup (250 mL): 155 Calories; 0.9 g Total Fat (0.2 g Mono, 0.3 g Poly, 0.1 g Sat); 0 mg Cholesterol;
30 g Carbohydrate; 10 g Fibre; 9 g Protein; 307 mg Sodium*

Pictured at right.

1. Roasted Chickpea Salad, page 15
2. Lentil Bulgur Pilaf, above
3. Carib-Beans And Rice, page 14

Props courtesy of: Cherison Enterprises
Pier 1 Imports

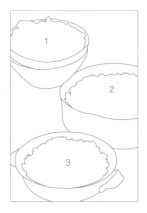

White Bean Gazpacho Salad

A delightful mixture of beans and crisp vegetables with classic gazpacho flavours. Serve with chicken, pork or seafood.

Can of diced tomatoes, drained	19 oz.	540 mL
Can of white kidney beans, rinsed and drained	19 oz.	540 mL
Diced English cucumber (with peel)	1 cup	250 mL
Diced yellow pepper	1 cup	250 mL
Finely diced onion	1/2 cup	125 mL
Olive oil	1/4 cup	60 mL
Red wine vinegar	2 tbsp.	30 mL
Liquid honey	1 tbsp.	15 mL
Chopped fresh cilantro	2 tsp.	10 mL
Lemon juice	2 tsp.	10 mL
Dried basil	1 tsp.	5 mL
Ground cumin	1 tsp.	5 mL
Garlic powder	1/4 tsp.	1 mL
Salt	1/2 tsp.	2 mL
Pepper	1/4 tsp.	1 mL

Combine first 5 ingredients in medium bowl.

Whisk remaining 10 ingredients in small bowl. Add to bean mixture. Toss. Chill, covered, for 1 hour, tossing occasionally, to blend flavours. Makes about 5 cups (1.25 L).

1 cup (250 mL): 235 Calories; 11.8 g Total Fat (8 g Mono, 1 g Poly, 1.5 g Sat); 0 mg Cholesterol; 26 g Carbohydrate; 6 g Fibre; 7 g Protein; 522 mg Sodium

Pictured at left.

1. Jicama Zucchini Salad, page 121
2. White Bean Gazpacho Salad, above
3. Bulgur Chickpea Curry, page 86

Props courtesy of: Mikasa Home Store
Stokes

BBQ Baked Beans

Some things are just better when you take them slow—which is why the slow cooker is the best place to cook perfectly tender, smoky and tangy baked beans.

Dried navy beans	2 cups	500 mL
Water	6 cups	1.5 L
Water	2 1/2 cups	625 mL
Cooking oil	1 tsp.	5 mL
Chopped onion	1 cup	250 mL
Garlic cloves, minced	2	2
(or 1/2 tsp., 2 mL, powder)		
Can of tomato sauce	14 oz.	398 mL
Brown sugar, packed	1/3 cup	75 mL
Apple cider vinegar	1/4 cup	60 mL
Bacon bits	1/4 cup	60 mL
Chili sauce	1/4 cup	60 mL
Dijon mustard	1 tbsp.	15 mL
Worcestershire sauce	1 tbsp.	15 mL
Salt	1 tsp.	5 mL
Pepper	1/2 tsp.	2 mL

Put beans into large bowl. Add first amount of water. Let stand, covered, for at least 8 hours or overnight. Drain. Rinse beans. Drain.

Put beans and second amount of water into 4 quart (4 L) slow cooker.

Heat cooking oil in small frying pan on medium. Add onion and garlic. Cook for 5 to 10 minutes, stirring occasionally, until onion is softened. Add to beans. Cook, covered, on Low for 7 to 8 hours or on High for 3 1/2 to 4 hours.

Combine remaining 9 ingredients in small bowl. Add to slow cooker. Stir. Cook, covered, on High for 1 hour. Makes about 7 cups (1.75 L).

1 cup (250 mL): 301 Calories; 2.4 g Total Fat (0.9 g Mono, 0.9 g Poly, 0.4 g Sat); 3 mg Cholesterol; 57 g Carbohydrate; 17 g Fibre; 16 g Protein; 1141 mg Sodium

Beans & Lentils

Black-Eyed Peas

We've added glitz and glam to this Southern staple with honey, Dijon mustard and snow peas. Best served with burgers, sausages or grilled meats.

Olive (or cooking) oil	2 tsp.	10 mL
Chopped onion	1 cup	250 mL
Diced celery	1 cup	250 mL
Garlic cloves, minced	2	2
(or 1/2 tsp., 2 mL, powder)		
Can of black-eyed peas, rinsed and drained	19 oz.	540 mL
Diced red pepper	1 cup	250 mL
Snow peas, trimmed and cut into thirds	6 oz.	170 g
Red wine vinegar	2 tbsp.	30 mL
Dijon mustard	1 tbsp.	15 mL
Liquid honey	1 tbsp.	15 mL
Salt	1/2 tsp.	2 mL
Pepper	1/4 tsp.	1 mL

Heat olive oil in large frying pan on medium. Add next 3 ingredients. Cook for 5 to 10 minutes, stirring occasionally, until onion is softened and starting to brown.

Add remaining 8 ingredients. Stir. Cook for about 5 minutes, stirring occasionally, until red pepper is tender-crisp. Makes about 6 cups (1.5 L).

1 cup (250 mL): 121 Calories; 2.4 g Total Fat (1.1 g Mono, 0.2 g Poly, 0.2 g Sat); 0 mg Cholesterol; 21 g Carbohydrate; 4 g Fibre; 6 g Protein; 263 mg Sodium

Pictured on page 89.

Beans & Lentils

Cranberry Lentil Salad

If you think tart and tangy cranberries go great with turkey, wait until you try them with soft lentils and crunchy walnuts. The light, refreshing dressing makes this a spectacular side for chicken, pork or fish.

Can of lentils, rinsed and drained	19 oz.	540 mL
Chopped walnuts, toasted (see Tip, page 128)	1/4 cup	60 mL
Dried cranberries	3 tbsp.	50 mL
Sliced green onion	2 tbsp.	30 mL
Frozen concentrated cranberry cocktail, thawed	3 tbsp.	50 mL
Olive (or cooking) oil	2 tbsp.	30 mL
Red wine vinegar	1 tbsp.	15 mL
Dijon mustard	1 tsp.	5 mL
Salt	1/4 tsp.	1 mL
Pepper	1/4 tsp.	1 mL

Combine first 4 ingredients in medium bowl.

Combine next 6 ingredients in jar with tight-fitting lid. Shake well. Drizzle over lentil mixture. Toss. Makes about 3 cups (750 mL).

1 cup (250 mL): 343 Calories; 15.6 g Total Fat (7.5 g Mono, 5.5 g Poly, 1.8 g Sat); 0 mg Cholesterol; 40 g Carbohydrate; 14 g Fibre; 13 g Protein; 425 mg Sodium

Microwave Lentils

Do you only use your microwave to heat up leftovers? Give this underappreciated appliance its chance to shine with this simple side that you can set and forget while a more complicated main course of chicken or pork keeps you occupied.

Prepared chicken broth	2 cups	500 mL
Dried red split lentils	1 cup	250 mL
Italian seasoning	1 tsp.	5 mL
Crumbled feta cheese	2 tbsp.	30 mL

(continued on next page)

Combine first 3 ingredients in large microwave-safe bowl. Microwave, covered, on high (100%) for 5 minutes. Stir. Microwave, covered, on medium (50%) for about 15 minutes until lentils are tender.

Sprinkle with cheese. Makes about 2 cups (500 mL).

1 cup (250 mL): 387 Calories; 5.2 g Total Fat (0.9 g Mono, 0.4 g Poly, 1.7 g Sat); 9 mg Cholesterol; 58 g Carbohydrate; 14 g Fibre; 29 g Protein; 1602 mg Sodium

---

Dijon Maple Baked Beans

Far removed from the camp-fire classic, these baked beans get an upscale makeover with the additions of sweet maple syrup, tangy Dijon mustard and earthy thyme. Perfect with pork chops or steak.

Chopped onion	1 1/2 cups	375 mL
Bacon slices, diced	4	4
Garlic cloves, minced,	2	2
(or 1/2 tsp., 2 mL powder)		
Cans of navy beans, rinsed and drained	3	3
(19 oz., 540 mL, each)		
Prepared chicken broth	1 cup	250 mL
Maple (or maple-flavoured) syrup	1/4 cup	60 mL
Dijon mustard	2 tbsp.	30 mL
Fancy (mild) molasses	2 tbsp.	30 mL
Dried thyme	3/4 tsp.	4 mL
Pepper	1/2 tsp.	2 mL

Heat large frying pan on medium. Add first 3 ingredients. Cook for about 10 minutes, stirring occasionally, until onion is softened.

Combine remaining 7 ingredients in 4 to 5 quart (4 to 5 L) slow cooker. Add bacon mixture. Stir. Cook, covered, on Low for 7 to 8 hours or on High for 3 1/2 to 4 hours. Makes about 5 1/2 cups (1.4 L).

1 cup (250 mL): 356 Calories; 3.4 g Total Fat (1.0 g Mono, 0.3 g Poly, 0.7 g Sat); 5 mg Cholesterol; 65 g Carbohydrate; 17 g Fibre; 18 g Protein; 487 mg Sodium

Savoury Stuffed Peppers

*If you're looking for a casual side, think stuffed—not stuffy—with this
down-home blend of lentils and rice packed into tender-crisp red pepper shells.*

Olive (or cooking) oil	1 tbsp.	15 mL
Finely chopped onion	1/2 cup	125 mL
Finely chopped fresh white mushrooms	3 cups	750 mL
Garlic cloves, minced	3	3
(or 3/4 tsp., 4 mL, powder)		
Prepared chicken broth	1 1/2 cups	375 mL
Dried red split lentils	1/3 cup	75 mL
White basmati rice	1/4 cup	60 mL
Grated Parmesan cheese	1/3 cup	75 mL
Dry (or alcohol-free) white wine	1/4 cup	60 mL
Finely chopped fresh parsley	1/4 cup	60 mL
(or 1 tbsp., 15 mL, flakes)		
Dried oregano	3/4 tsp.	4 mL
Pepper	1/4 tsp.	1 mL
Small red peppers, halved lengthwise	3	3
Grated Parmesan cheese	2 tbsp.	30 mL
Finely chopped fresh parsley	1 tbsp.	15 mL

Heat olive oil in large saucepan on medium-high. Add onion. Cook for 2 to
4 minutes, stirring often, until starting to soften. Add mushrooms and garlic.
Cook for about 5 minutes, stirring occasionally, until liquid is evaporated.

Add next 3 ingredients. Stir. Bring to a boil. Reduce heat to medium-low.
Simmer, covered, for about 20 minutes, without stirring, until rice is
tender. Transfer to medium bowl. Let stand for 10 minutes.

Add next 5 ingredients. Stir.

Spoon lentil mixture into red pepper halves. Arrange in greased 9 × 13 inch
(22 × 33 cm) pan. Sprinkle with second amount of cheese. Cover with greased
foil. Bake in 350°F (175°C) oven for 30 minutes. Remove foil. Bake for
about 15 minutes until cheese is melted and red peppers are tender-crisp.

Sprinkle with parsley. Makes 6 stuffed peppers.

*1 stuffed pepper: 167 Calories; 5.6 g Total Fat (1.8 g Mono, 0.4 g Poly, 1.6 g Sat); 6 mg Cholesterol;
20 g Carbohydrate; 3 g Fibre; 9 g Protein; 532 mg Sodium*

Pictured on page 35.

Tomato Pesto Biscotti

*These savoury biscotti are miles away from the neighbourhood
coffee shop. Dunk them in soup or stew, pair with a salad,
serve as an appetizer or give a batch as a hostess gift.*

All-purpose flour	2 cups	500 mL
Baking powder	1/2 tsp.	2 mL
Italian seasoning	1/2 tsp.	2 mL
Salt	1/4 tsp.	1 mL
Pepper	1/4 tsp.	1 mL
Butter (or hard margarine), softened	1/4 cup	60 mL
Granulated sugar	1/4 cup	60 mL
Large eggs	2	2
Sun-dried tomato pesto	1/4 cup	60 mL

Measure first 5 ingredients into large bowl. Stir. Make a well in centre.

Cream butter and sugar in small bowl. Add eggs, 1 at a time, beating well
after each addition. Stir in pesto until combined. Add to well. Mix until
soft dough forms. Turn out onto lightly floured surface. Knead 6 times.
Divide dough in half. Shape each half into 8 inch (20 cm) long log.
Place logs crosswise on greased large baking sheet about 3 inches
(7.5 cm) apart. Flatten logs slightly. Bake in 350°F (175°C) oven for
about 20 minutes until edges are golden. Let stand on baking sheet
for about 10 minutes until cool enough to handle. Using serrated knife,
cut logs diagonally into 1/2 inch (12 mm) thick slices. Arrange, evenly
spaced apart, on greased large baking sheet. Reduce heat to 275°F (140°C).
Bake for 20 minutes. Turn slices over. Turn oven off. Let stand in oven for
about 30 minutes until dry and crisp. Makes about 18 biscotti.

*1 biscotti: 87 Calories; 3.1 g Total Fat (0.9 g Mono, 0.2 g Poly, 1.8 g Sat); 27 mg Cholesterol;
13 g Carbohydrate; trace Fibre; 2 g Protein; 99 mg Sodium*

Pictured on page 126 and back cover.

Greek-Style Flatbread

These pita-like flatbreads may not have pockets, but they've got something better—a soft, white texture and a great flavour that's delicious on its own or with curries, stews, soups or salads.

All-purpose flour	4 cups	1 L
Granulated sugar	1 tbsp.	15 mL
Warm water	1/2 cup	125 mL
Envelope of active dry yeast (or 2 1/4 tsp., 11 mL)	1/4 oz.	8 g
Warm water	1 cup	250 mL
Salt	2 tsp.	10 mL
Olive oil	1 tbsp.	15 mL
Olive oil	2 tbsp.	30 mL

Measure flour into large bowl. Make a well in centre.

Combine sugar and first amount of warm water in small bowl. Sprinkle yeast over top. Let stand for 10 minutes. Stir to dissolve yeast. Add to well.

Measure second amount of warm water and salt into same small bowl. Stir until dissolved. Add to well. Add first amount of olive oil. Mix until soft dough forms. Turn out onto lightly floured surface. Knead for about 10 minutes until smooth and elastic. Place in greased large bowl, turning once to grease top. Cover with greased waxed paper and tea towel. Let stand in oven with light on and door closed for about 1 hour until doubled in bulk. Place ungreased baking sheet on lowest rack in 500°F (260°C) oven. Punch dough down. Turn out onto lightly floured surface. Knead for about 1 minute until smooth. Divide dough into 12 equal pieces. Work with 1 piece at a time. Cover remaining pieces with tea towel to prevent drying. Roll each piece into 5 inch (12.5 cm) diameter circle on lightly floured surface.

Brush circles with second amount of olive oil. Place 3 circles, oil-side down, on hot baking sheet. Brush tops with olive oil. Bake on lowest rack in 500°F (260°C) oven for about 3 minutes until golden on bottom. Turn. Bake for about 2 minutes until bottom is golden. Remove to towel-lined tray. Cover to keep warm. Repeat with remaining circles. Serve warm (see Note). Makes 12 flatbreads.

(continued on next page)

1 flatbread: 169 Calories; 3.4 g Total Fat (2.5 g Mono, 0.3 g Poly, 0.5 g Sat); 0 mg Cholesterol; 31 g Carbohydrate; 1 g Fibre; 4 g Protein; 390 mg Sodium

Pictured on page 36.

Note: To store, wrap each flatbread individually in plastic wrap and place all in a large freezer bag. Store for up to 1 month in freezer. To reheat, wrap frozen flatbreads in foil and place in 350°F (175°C) oven for 10 to 15 minutes.

Parmesan Yorkshire Pudding

This traditional British roast beef side has been given a good dose of Italian Parmesan flair.

Cooking oil	2 tbsp.	30 mL
Large eggs	3	3
Milk	1 cup	250 mL
Grated Parmesan cheese	1/3 cup	75 mL
Salt	1/4 tsp.	1 mL
All-purpose flour	1 cup	250 mL

Put cooking oil into 9 × 9 inch (22 × 22 cm) pan. Heat in 425°F (220°C) oven for about 10 minutes until hot.

Whisk next 4 ingredients in medium bowl. Add flour. Whisk until smooth. Pour into hot pan. Bake for about 10 minutes until starting to puff. Reduce heat to 350°F (175°C). Bake for about 40 minutes until browned. Serve immediately. Cuts into 6 pieces.

1 piece: 187 Calories; 9.2 g Total Fat (3.8 g Mono, 1.7 g Poly, 2.2 g Sat); 99 mg Cholesterol; 17 g Carbohydrate; trace Fibre; 9 g Protein; 259 mg Sodium

Pumpkin Sage Biscuits

*Think pumpkin's just for pies? The prince of the patch adds tenderness
and moisture to these sage and onion-speckled biscuits with no oil
or eggs required! Serve with soup, salad, roast pork or chicken.*

Biscuit mix	2 3/4 cups	675 mL
Dried sage	1 tsp.	5 mL
Garlic powder	1/4 tsp.	1 mL
Canned pure pumpkin (no spices), see Tip, below	3/4 cup	175 mL
Finely chopped green onion	1/2 cup	125 mL
Milk	1/2 cup	125 mL
Biscuit mix	2 tbsp.	30 mL

Measure first 3 ingredients into medium bowl. Stir. Make a well in centre.

Combine next 3 ingredients in small bowl. Add to well. Stir until soft
dough forms.

Sprinkle second amount of biscuit mix on work surface. Turn out dough
onto biscuit mix. Roll gently to coat. Roll or pat out to 1/2 inch (12 mm)
thickness. Cut into 2 inch (5 cm) circles with lightly floured biscuit cutter.
Arrange, about 1 inch (2.5 cm) apart, on greased baking sheet. Roll scraps
and repeat. Bake in 450°F (230°C) oven for 12 to 15 minutes until lightly
browned. Makes about 20 biscuits.

*1 biscuit: 157 Calories; 6.4 g Total Fat (2.7 g Mono, 0.6 g Poly, 1.8 g Sat); 1 mg Cholesterol;
22 g Carbohydrate; 1 g Fibre; 3 g Protein; 392 mg Sodium*

 tip Store any leftover pumpkin in an airtight container in the refrigerator
for 3 to 5 days or in the freezer for up to 12 months.

Herb Spiral Bread

A crusty golden loaf with a twist—literally! A spicy swirl adds
flavour and prettiness to this easy, yet impressive-looking, loaf.

Frozen white bread dough, covered, thawed in refrigerator overnight	1	1
Butter (or hard margarine), melted	2 tbsp.	30 mL
Italian seasoning	1 tbsp.	15 mL
Coarse salt	1 tsp.	5 mL

Roll or pat out dough on lightly floured surface to 12 × 14 inch (30 × 35 cm) rectangle. Brush with melted butter.

Combine Italian seasoning and salt in small bowl. Sprinkle over dough. Press down lightly. Roll up, jelly roll-style, from short side. Pinch seam against roll to seal. Transfer to greased 9 × 5 × 3 inch (22 × 12.5 × 7.5 cm) loaf pan. Cover with greased waxed paper and tea towel. Let stand in oven with light on and door closed for about 1 1/2 hours until doubled in bulk. Bake in 350°F (175°C) oven for about 30 minutes until golden brown and hollow sounding when tapped. Makes one 8 1/2 inch (21 cm) loaf. Cuts into 16 slices.

1 slice: 92 Calories; 2.6 g Total Fat (0.4 g Mono, 0.1 g Poly, 0.9 g Sat); 4 mg Cholesterol; 14 g Carbohydrate; 1 g Fibre; 3 g Protein; 289 mg Sodium

Paré Pointer
Banks can't keep secrets—too many tellers.

Sourdough Stuffing Muffins

Your guests won't be able to say they've had this side before!
Impress them all with your creativity when you serve up this stuffing
muffin packed with sage, onion, bacon and the great flavour
of sourdough. Serve with roast chicken or pork.

Finely chopped onion	1 cup	250 mL
Bacon slices, diced	4	4
Garlic clove, minced	1	1
(or 1/4 tsp., 1 mL, powder)		
Large eggs	3	3
Milk	1 1/2 cups	375 mL
Salt	1 tsp.	5 mL
Pepper	1/2 tsp.	2 mL
Dried sage	1/4 tsp.	1 mL
Cubed sourdough bread	3 cups	750 mL
Finely chopped walnuts, toasted	1/2 cup	125 mL
(see Tip, page 128)		
Yellow cornmeal	1/4 cup	60 mL

Heat small frying pan on medium. Add first 3 ingredients. Cook for
5 to 10 minutes, stirring occasionally, until bacon is almost crisp. Drain.
Transfer to large plate. Spread evenly. Cool.

Beat next 5 ingredients in large bowl until combined.

Add bread cubes, walnuts and bacon mixture. Stir until bread is coated.
Let stand for 10 minutes.

Sprinkle cornmeal into 12 greased muffin cups. Turn muffin pan to coat
bottom and sides of cups with cornmeal. Spoon bread mixture into muffin
cups. Bake in 375°F (190°C) oven for about 30 minutes until browned and
wooden pick inserted in centre of muffin comes out clean. Run knife
around inside edges of cups to loosen muffins. Serve immediately.
Makes 12 muffins.

1 muffin: 146 Calories; 6.5 g Total Fat (1.5 g Mono, 2.7 g Poly, 1.5 g Sat); 50 mg Cholesterol;
17 g Carbohydrate; 2 g Fibre; 6 g Protein; 323 mg Sodium

Florentine Squares

The taste of a spinach quiche in a handy bread form.
This filling little side goes well with a soup or salad.

All-purpose flour	2 1/2 cups	625 mL
Grated Swiss cheese	1 cup	250 mL
Bacon bits	3 tbsp.	50 mL
Granulated sugar	1 tbsp.	15 mL
Baking powder	2 tsp.	10 mL
Ground nutmeg	3/4 tsp.	4 mL
Salt	3/4 tsp.	4 mL
Baking soda	1/2 tsp.	2 mL
Large eggs	2	2
Box of frozen chopped spinach, thawed and squeezed dry	10 oz.	300 g
Buttermilk (or soured milk, see Tip, below)	1 cup	250 mL
Cooking oil	1/3 cup	75 mL

Measure first 8 ingredients into large bowl. Stir. Make a well in centre.

Combine remaining 4 ingredients in medium bowl. Add to well. Stir until just moistened. Batter will be thick. Spread in greased 9 × 13 inch (22 × 33 cm) pan. Bake in 375°F (190°C) oven for about 25 minutes until wooden pick inserted in centre comes out clean. Cuts into 12 squares.

1 square: 211 Calories; 10.2 g Total Fat (4.2 g Mono, 2.0 g Poly, 2.6 g Sat); 41 mg Cholesterol; 22 g Carbohydrate; 2 g Fibre; 8 g Protein; 367 mg Sodium

 tip To make soured milk, measure 1 tbsp. (15 mL) white vinegar or lemon juice into a 1 cup (250 mL) liquid measure. Add enough milk to make 1 cup (250 mL). Stir. Let stand for 1 minute.

Easy Onion Buns

If you've always wanted to make bread from scratch but weren't sure about all that kneading and shaping, this recipe has a quick yeast-risen dough that requires neither! It's loaded with the savoury flavours of caramelized onion and thyme.

Butter (or hard margarine)	2 tbsp.	30 mL
Chopped onion	2/3 cup	150 mL
Hot water	1 cup	250 mL
Butter (or hard margarine), melted	1/4 cup	60 mL
Granulated sugar	2 tbsp.	30 mL
Salt	1 1/2 tsp.	7 mL
All-purpose flour	2 cups	500 mL
Envelope of instant yeast	1/4 oz.	8 g
(or 2 1/4 tsp., 11 mL)		
Chopped fresh thyme	2 tsp.	10 mL
(or 1/2 tsp., 2 mL, dried, see Note)		

Melt first amount of butter in small frying pan. Add onion. Cook for about 10 minutes, stirring occasionally, until caramelized. Set aside.

Measure next 4 ingredients into large bowl. Stir until sugar is dissolved. Liquid should still be very warm.

Combine remaining 3 ingredients in small bowl. Add to melted butter mixture. Stir briskly until flour is moistened and sticky batter forms. Stir in onion. Scrape sides of dough down into bowl. Cover with greased plastic wrap. Let stand at room temperature for about 30 minutes until almost doubled in bulk. Stir dough down with spoon. Fill 12 well-greased muffin cups half full. Cover with greased plastic wrap. Let stand in oven with light on and door closed for about 30 minutes until dough rises above tops of muffin cups. Remove and discard plastic wrap. Bake in 375°F (190°C) oven for 18 to 20 minutes until golden brown. Makes 12 buns.

1 bun: 131 Calories; 5.7 g Total Fat (1.5 g Mono, 0.2 g Poly, 3.6 g Sat); 15 mg Cholesterol; 18 g Carbohydrate; 1 g Fibre; 2 g Protein; 334 mg Sodium

Pictured on page 36.

Note: If using dried thyme, cook with onion.

Caraway Beer Muffins

A buttery crust forms over these firm, savoury muffins. Serve alongside bratwurst and sauerkraut with German mustard. You can also fill them with ham and cheese for a delicious lunch sandwich!

All-purpose flour	1 3/4 cups	425 mL
Rye flour	3/4 cup	175 mL
Granulated sugar	2 tbsp.	30 mL
Baking powder	1 tbsp.	15 mL
Caraway seed	1 tsp.	5 mL
Salt	1/2 tsp.	2 mL
Can of beer (or alcohol-free)	12 1/2 oz.	355 mL
Butter (or hard margarine), melted	1/4 cup	60 mL

Measure first 6 ingredients into large bowl. Stir. Make a well in centre.

Add beer to well. Stir until just moistened. Spray 12 muffin cups with cooking spray. Fill 2/3 full.

Drizzle muffins with melted butter. Bake in 375°F (190°C) oven for 20 to 22 minutes until wooden pick inserted in centre of muffin comes out clean. Let stand in pan for 5 minutes. Run knife around inside edges of cups to loosen muffins. Remove muffins from pan and place on wire rack to cool. Makes 12 muffins.

1 muffin: 138 Calories; 3.9 g Total Fat (1.0 g Mono, 0.2 g Poly, 2.4 g Sat); 10 mg Cholesterol; 21 g Carbohydrate; 1 g Fibre; 2 g Protein; 190 mg Sodium

Paré Pointer
Combine a chef and a baseball player and you'll get a better batter.

Olive Soda Bread

*For those who go ga-ga over olives, this fresh take on an old favourite
is a must-have accompaniment. For variation, use kalamata olives
for black olives, or pimiento-stuffed olives in place of green olives.*

All-purpose flour	2 cups	500 mL
Baking soda	1 tsp.	5 mL
Salt	3/4 tsp.	4 mL
Buttermilk (or soured milk, see Tip, page 31)	1 cup	250 mL
Chopped sliced black olives	2 tbsp.	30 mL
Chopped sliced green olives	2 tbsp.	30 mL
Olive (or cooking) oil	2 tbsp.	30 mL

Measure first 3 ingredients into large bowl. Stir. Make a well in centre.

Add remaining 4 ingredients to well. Stir until almost combined. Turn out
onto lightly floured surface. Knead 6 to 8 times until soft dough forms.
Gently pat dough into 6 inch (15 cm) circle. Place dough on greased
baking sheet. Cut '+' on top of dough, making cuts about 5 inches
(12.5 cm) long and 1/2 inch (12 mm) deep, using sharp knife. Bake
in 400°F (205°C) oven for about 30 minutes until wooden pick inserted
in centre comes out clean. Let stand for 5 minutes. Cuts into 8 wedges.

*1 wedge: 149 Calories; 4.4 g Total Fat (3.1 g Mono, 0.4 g Poly, 0.7 g Sat); 1 mg Cholesterol;
24 g Carbohydrate; 1 g Fibre; 4 g Protein; 483 mg Sodium*

Pictured at right.

1. Savoury Stuffed Peppers, page 24
2. Olive Soda Bread, above

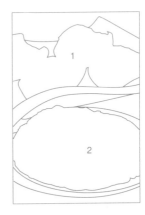

Breads

Bread Sticks

*These golden, crisp bread sticks flecked with cheese and herbs are
simply brimming with personality. Serve with salad, soup or pasta.*

Frozen unbaked dinner rolls, covered, thawed in refrigerator overnight	12	12
Butter (or hard margarine), melted	3 tbsp.	50 mL
Grated Parmesan cheese	3/4 cup	175 mL
Dried basil	1 tsp.	5 mL
Dried oregano	1/2 tsp.	2 mL
Pepper	1/2 tsp.	2 mL

Roll each dough piece into 8 inch (20 cm) long stick. Arrange on
parchment paper-lined baking sheet. Brush with melted butter.

Combine remaining 4 ingredients in small bowl. Sprinkle over sticks.
Bake in 375°F (190°C) oven for about 15 minutes until browned.
Makes 12 sticks.

*1 stick: 162 Calories; 6.4 g Total Fat (0.7 g Mono, 0.1 g Poly, 2.8 g Sat); 13 mg Cholesterol;
18 g Carbohydrate; 2 g Fibre; 7 g Protein; 357 mg Sodium*

Pictured at left.

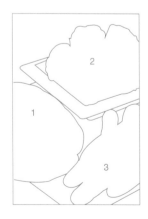

1. Greek-Style Flatbread, page 26
2. Easy Onion Buns, page 32
3. Bread Sticks, above

Props courtesy of: Stokes

Tomato Ricotta Penne

Perfect for olive lovers, this cheese-coated penne is sure to please.
Goes great with chicken or fish.

Water	8 cups	2 L
Salt	1 tsp.	5 mL
Penne pasta	2 cups	500 mL
Olive (or cooking) oil	1 tsp.	5 mL
Chopped onion	1 cup	250 mL
Garlic cloves, minced	2	2
Chopped red pepper	1 cup	250 mL
Chopped, pitted kalamata olives	3 tbsp.	50 mL
Sun-dried tomato pesto	1 tbsp.	15 mL
Salt	1/4 tsp.	1 mL
Pepper	1/4 tsp.	1 mL
Block of cream cheese, softened	4 oz.	125 g
Ricotta cheese	1/2 cup	125 mL
Chopped fresh parsley	1 tbsp.	15 mL

Combine water and salt in large saucepan or Dutch oven. Bring to a boil. Add pasta. Boil, uncovered, for 14 to 16 minutes, stirring occasionally, until tender but firm. Drain, reserving 1/4 cup (60 mL) cooking water. Return pasta to same pot. Cover to keep warm.

Heat olive oil in medium saucepan on medium. Add onion and garlic. Cook for 5 to 10 minutes, stirring often, until onion is softened.

Add next 5 ingredients. Cook for 3 to 5 minutes, stirring occasionally, until red pepper is tender-crisp.

Mash cream cheese and ricotta cheese with fork in small bowl. Add to red pepper mixture. Heat and stir for about 1 minute until heated through and creamy. Add reserved cooking water. Stir. Add to pasta. Toss until coated.

Sprinkle with parsley. Makes about 4 cups (1 L).

1 cup (250 mL): 414 Calories; 17.6 g Total Fat (5.7 g Mono, 0.8 g Poly, 9.2 g Sat); 47 mg Cholesterol; 50 g Carbohydrate; 3 g Fibre; 14 g Protein; 301 mg Sodium

Fusilli Rosa

*Tri-colour pasta speckled with zucchini and tomato make for
a visual feast. Coated in a creamy, three-cheese sauce, this side
just may outshine your entree. Use fresh herbs for best results.*

Water	8 cups	2 L
Salt	1 tsp.	5 mL
Tri-colour fusilli pasta	3 cups	750 mL
Olive (or cooking) oil	1 tbsp.	15 mL
Diced zucchini (with peel)	1 cup	250 mL
Sliced leek (white part only)	1 cup	250 mL
Garlic clove, minced	1	1
(or 1/4 tsp., 1 mL, powder)		
Can of diced tomatoes (with juice)	14 oz.	398 mL
Half-and-half cream	1/3 cup	75 mL
Chopped fresh basil	2 tbsp.	30 mL
Chopped fresh oregano	1 tbsp.	15 mL
Grated Asiago cheese	1/4 cup	60 mL

Combine water and salt in Dutch oven. Bring to a boil. Add pasta. Boil,
uncovered, for 7 to 9 minutes, stirring occasionally, until tender but firm.
Drain. Return to same pot. Cover to keep warm.

Heat olive oil in large frying pan on medium. Add next 3 ingredients.
Cook for about 5 minutes, stirring occasionally, until leek is softened
and zucchini is tender-crisp.

Add tomatoes with juice. Stir. Bring to a boil. Reduce heat to medium-low.
Cook, uncovered, for 2 to 4 minutes until heated through.

Add next 3 ingredients. Heat and stir for 1 minute. Add to pasta.
Toss until coated. Transfer to serving bowl.

Sprinkle with cheese. Makes about 5 cups (1.25 L).

*1 cup (250 mL): 618 Calories; 8.9 g Total Fat (2.9 g Mono, 1.8 g Poly, 3.1 g Sat); 11 mg Cholesterol;
116 g Carbohydrate; 5 g Fibre; 22 g Protein; 296 mg Sodium*

Asian Noodle Salad

*Toss some chicken or pork onto the grill, then toss together this
easy and refreshing Vietnamese-inspired salad. It'll make
an easy supper for a warm summer evening.*

Rice vermicelli, broken up	12 oz.	340 g
Bean sprouts	1 cup	250 mL
Grated carrot	1/2 cup	125 mL
Julienned English cucumber (with peel), see Tip, page 113	1/2 cup	125 mL
Thinly sliced red pepper	1/2 cup	125 mL
Thinly sliced green onion	1/4 cup	60 mL
Chopped fresh mint	2 tbsp.	30 mL
Fish sauce	1 1/2 tbsp.	25 mL
Lime juice	1 tbsp.	15 mL
Liquid honey	1 tbsp.	15 mL
Sweet chili sauce	1 tbsp.	15 mL
Sesame oil (for flavour)	1 tsp.	5 mL
Chili paste (sambal oelek)	1/2 tsp.	2 mL
Unsalted peanuts, coarsely chopped	1/4 cup	60 mL
Chopped fresh cilantro	2 tbsp.	30 mL

Put vermicelli into large heatproof bowl. Cover with boiling water. Let stand
for about 5 minutes until tender. Drain. Rinse with cold water until cool.
Drain well. Transfer to large bowl.

Add next 6 ingredients. Toss.

Whisk next 6 ingredients in small bowl. Drizzle over vermicelli mixture. Toss.

Sprinkle with peanuts and cilantro. Makes about 6 cups (1.5 L).

*1 cup (250 mL): 271 Calories; 3.9 g Total Fat (1.8 g Mono, 1.3 g Poly, 0.6 g Sat); 0 mg Cholesterol;
53 g Carbohydrate; 2 g Fibre; 8 g Protein; 359 mg Sodium*

Pictured on page 71.

Pasta & Noodles

Tabbouleh

*Tabbouleh is a traditional Lebanese salad that is as delicious as it is easy.
It's usually made with bulgur, but it's faster and just as good with couscous.
An excellent side or serve on its own with romaine leaves or pita chips.*

Water	1/2 cup	125 mL
Couscous	1/2 cup	125 mL
Finely diced English cucumber (with peel)	3/4 cup	175 mL
Finely diced Roma (plum) tomato, seeds removed	3/4 cup	175 mL
Finely diced red pepper	1/2 cup	125 mL
Finely chopped fresh parsley	1/3 cup	75 mL
Finely chopped fresh mint	1/4 cup	60 mL
Finely chopped green onion	1/4 cup	60 mL
Finely diced red onion	1/4 cup	60 mL
Olive oil	1/3 cup	75 mL
Lemon juice	1/4 cup	60 mL
Ground cinnamon	1/4 tsp.	1 mL
Ground cumin	1/8 tsp.	0.5 mL
Salt	1/2 tsp.	2 mL
Pepper	1/8 tsp.	0.5 mL

Measure water into medium saucepan. Bring to a boil. Add couscous. Stir. Remove from heat. Let stand, covered, for about 5 minutes until water is absorbed. Fluff with fork. Transfer to large bowl. Cool completely.

Add next 7 ingredients. Stir gently.

Combine remaining 6 ingredients in jar with tight-fitting lid. Shake well. Add to couscous mixture. Stir. Chill, covered, for at least 1 hour or up to 8 hours before serving. Makes about 4 cups (1 L).

*1 cup (250 mL): 263 Calories; 17.5 g Total Fat (12.7 g Mono, 1.6 g Poly, 2.4 g Sat);
0 mg Cholesterol; 24 g Carbohydrate; 2 g Fibre; 4 g Protein; 302 mg Sodium*

Pictured on page 126 and back cover.

Orzo Confetti

*Italian-spiced pasta that cooks in your microwave for an easy one-pot meal—
now that's something to celebrate! Heat the party up with your favourite
entree—this pleasing pasta goes with just about anything!*

Orzo	1 cup	250 mL
Sliced fresh white mushrooms	1 cup	250 mL
Diced celery	1/2 cup	125 mL
Diced onion	1/2 cup	125 mL
Diced red pepper	1/2 cup	125 mL
Garlic powder	1/2 tsp.	2 mL
Italian seasoning	1/2 tsp.	2 mL
Salt	1/2 tsp.	2 mL
Pepper	1/4 tsp.	1 mL
Prepared vegetable broth	2 cups	500 mL

Combine first 9 ingredients in medium microwave-safe bowl. Add broth.
Stir. Microwave, covered, on high (100%) for about 20 minutes, stirring
every 5 minutes, until orzo is tender and liquid is absorbed. Makes about
4 cups (1 L).

*1 cup (250 mL): 107 Calories; 0.2 g Total Fat (trace Mono, 0.1 g Poly, trace Sat); 0 mg Cholesterol;
24 g Carbohydrate; 1 g Fibre; 3 g Protein; 784 mg Sodium*

Sesame Chow Mein

*That's using your noodle! Think smart and serve this versatile,
quick and easy noodle dish with beef, chicken or pork.*

Prepared chicken broth	1 cup	250 mL
Water	2/3 cup	150 mL
Sesame oil (for flavour)	1 tbsp.	15 mL
Soy sauce	1 tbsp.	15 mL
Pepper	1/4 tsp.	1 mL
Frozen cut green beans	1 cup	250 mL
Fresh, thin Chinese-style egg noodles	8 oz.	225 g
Sesame seeds, toasted (see Tip, page 128)	1 tbsp.	15 mL

(continued on next page)

Combine first 5 ingredients in large frying pan. Bring to a boil on medium-high. Add green beans. Cook, covered, for 1 minute.

Add noodles. Stir. Cook, covered, for 2 to 4 minutes until noodles are softened. Heat and stir for about 1 minute until all liquid is absorbed.

Sprinkle with sesame seeds. Makes about 3 1/3 cups (825 mL).

1 cup (250 mL): 268 Calories; 6.4 g Total Fat (2.3 g Mono, 2.4 g Poly, 0.9 g Sat); 6 mg Cholesterol; 42 g Carbohydrate; 3 g Fibre; 11 g Protein; 826 mg Sodium

Skillet Mac And Cheese

You could make macaroni 'n' cheese from a box... but why?
Our version of this cheesy classic is just as easy and a whole lot tastier.

Butter (or hard margarine)	2 tbsp.	30 mL
Finely chopped green pepper	1/4 cup	60 mL
Finely chopped onion	1/4 cup	60 mL
Dry mustard	1/4 tsp.	1 mL
Salt	1/2 tsp.	2 mL
Pepper	1/8 tsp.	0.5 mL
Elbow macaroni	1 1/2 cups	375 mL
Milk	1 cup	250 mL
Water	1 cup	250 mL
Grated sharp Cheddar cheese	1 1/2 cups	375 mL

Melt butter in medium frying pan on medium. Add next 5 ingredients. Cook for about 5 minutes, stirring occasionally, until onion is to softened.

Add next 3 ingredients. Bring to a boil. Reduce heat to medium-low. Cook, partially covered, for about 10 minutes, stirring occasionally, until pasta is tender but firm.

Add cheese. Stir until melted. Makes about 2 1/2 cups (625 mL).

1 cup (250 mL): 639 Calories; 33.6 g Total Fat (9.1 g Mono, 1.4 g Poly, 20.8 g Sat); 99 mg Cholesterol; 55 g Carbohydrate; 2 g Fibre; 29 g Protein; 1013 mg Sodium

Butternut Squash Gnocchi

*Tuck yourself into these comforting "pillows" of nutmeg-scented
butternut squash gnocchi (pronounced NOH-kee). A gentle toss
in a little butter and Parmesan cheese is all that's needed
to bring out their naturally sweet, delicate flavours.*

Unpeeled baking potatoes (about 2 medium)	1 lb.	454 g
Egg yolk (large), fork-beaten	1	1
Mashed butternut squash	1 cup	250 mL
(about 1 lb, 454 g, uncooked)		
Salt	1 tsp.	5 mL
Ground nutmeg	1/4 tsp.	1 mL
All-purpose flour	2 cups	500 mL
Water	12 cups	3 L
Salt	1 1/2 tsp.	7 mL
Butter (or hard margarine), melted	2 tbsp.	30 mL
Grated Parmesan cheese	1/4 cup	60 mL

Prick potatoes in several places with a fork. Wrap individually with paper
towels. Microwave on high (100%) for 10 to 15 minutes, turning at
halftime, until tender. Wrap in tea towel. Let stand for 10 minutes. Unwrap.
Let stand for about 10 minutes until cool enough to handle. Peel. Transfer
to large bowl. Mash.

Add next 4 ingredients. Stir well. Add flour, 1/2 cup (125 mL) at a time,
stirring with fork until soft dough forms. Knead in bowl 8 to 10 times
until flour is absorbed. Divide dough into 4 equal portions. Roll each
portion on lightly floured surface into 16 inch (40 cm) rope. Cut each
rope into 1/2 inch (12 mm) pieces.

Combine water and salt in Dutch oven. Bring to a boil. Add half of gnocchi.
Boil, uncovered, for 4 to 5 minutes, stirring occasionally, until gnocchi float
to surface. Remove with slotted spoon to serving dish. Cover to keep warm.
Repeat with remaining gnocchi.

Drizzle with melted butter. Sprinkle with cheese. Toss gently. Makes about
4 cups (1 L).

*1 cup (250 mL): 442 Calories; 9.5 g Total Fat (2.6 g Mono, 0.8 g Poly, 5.4 g Sat); 71 mg Cholesterol;
77 g Carbohydrate; 5 g Fibre; 13 g Protein; 750 mg Sodium*

Creamy Tomato Orzo

Is it rice? Is it pasta? Tender rice-shaped grains of orzo pasta combine the best of both worlds, especially when blanketed in a luscious tomato cream. Serve with beef, chicken, pork or fish.

Prepared chicken broth	2 cups	500 mL
Water	2 cups	500 mL
Orzo	1 1/4 cups	300 mL
Olive (or cooking) oil	1 tbsp.	15 mL
Finely chopped onion	1/4 cup	60 mL
Garlic cloves, minced	2	2
(or 1/2 tsp., 2 mL, powder)		
Canned diced tomatoes, drained	1 cup	250 mL
Half-and-half cream	2/3 cup	150 mL
Frozen peas	1/2 cup	125 mL
Grated Parmesan cheese	2/3 cup	150 mL
Salt	1/8 tsp.	0.5 mL
Pepper	1/4 tsp.	1 mL
Finely chopped fresh basil	2 tbsp.	30 mL
Grated Parmesan cheese, for garnish		

Combine chicken broth and water in large saucepan or Dutch oven. Bring to a boil. Add pasta. Boil, uncovered, for about 8 minutes, stirring occasionally, until tender but firm. Drain, reserving 1/4 cup (60 mL) cooking water. Return pasta to same pot. Cover to keep warm.

Heat olive oil in large frying pan on medium-high. Add onion and garlic. Cook for about 2 minutes, stirring often, until onion is softened. Add tomatoes. Cook for about 8 minutes, stirring occasionally, until liquid is evaporated.

Add cream and peas. Stir. Add next 3 ingredients and pasta. Heat and stir for about 2 minutes, adding reserved cooking water, 1 tbsp. (15 mL) at a time, until desired consistency.

Sprinkle with basil. Garnish with cheese. Makes about 5 cups (1.25 L).

1 cup (250 mL): 229 Calories; 10.1 g Total Fat (4.1 g Mono, 0.5 g Poly, 5.0 g Sat); 21 mg Cholesterol; 25 g Carbohydrate; 1 g Fibre; 9 g Protein; 448 mg Sodium

Sesame Soba Noodles

When it comes to Asian cooking, simple is where it's at. Just toss tender Japanese buckwheat noodles with sesame, chili and soy and you'll have a delicious dish to serve with stir-fries, grilled beef, chicken or pork.

Water	8 cups	2 L
Salt	1 tsp.	5 mL
Soba noodles	6 oz.	170 g
Soy sauce	2 tbsp.	30 mL
Sesame oil (for flavour)	1 tbsp.	15 mL
Dried crushed chilies	1/8 tsp.	0.5 mL
Sesame seeds, toasted (see Tip, page 128)	2 tsp.	10 mL

Combine water and salt in Dutch oven. Bring to a boil. Add noodles. Boil, uncovered, for about 5 minutes, stirring occasionally, until tender but firm. Drain. Return to same pot.

Add next 3 ingredients. Toss.

Sprinkle with sesame seeds. Makes about 3 cups (750 mL).

1 cup (250 mL): 258 Calories; 6 g Total Fat (2.7 g Mono, 2.8 g Poly, 0.8 g Sat); 0 mg Cholesterol; 45 g Carbohydrate; 3 g Fibre; 7 g Protein; 883 mg Sodium

Basil Cream Fettuccine

We're big fans of one-pot dishes—they mean only one pot to look after and, better still, only one to wash! Pasta and a creamy, lemony sauce come together easily in your Dutch oven.

Water	12 cups	3 L
Salt	1 1/2 tsp.	7 mL
Fettuccine	8 oz.	225 g
Half-and-half cream	1 cup	250 mL
Grated Parmesan cheese	1/2 cup	125 mL
Butter (or hard margarine)	2 tbsp.	30 mL
Chopped fresh basil	1/4 cup	60 mL
Lemon juice	2 tsp.	10 mL

(continued on next page)

Combine water and salt in large saucepan or Dutch oven. Bring to a boil. Add pasta. Boil, uncovered, for 12 to 15 minutes, stirring occasionally, until tender but firm. Drain. Return to same pot.

Add next 3 ingredients. Heat and stir on medium until thickened. Remove from heat.

Add basil and lemon juice. Toss. Serve immediately. Makes about 2 1/2 cups (625 mL).

1 cup (250 mL): 628 Calories; 27.4 g Total Fat (7.3 g Mono, 0.9 g Poly, 16.8 g Sat); 75 mg Cholesterol; 73 g Carbohydrate; 3 g Fibre; 24 g Protein; 481 mg Sodium

Chili Lime Noodles

Take your senses on a flavour adventure! Your taste buds will be warmed by hot chili, soothed by brown sugar sweetness, and refreshed by cool lime. Don't forget to bring a main course of grilled beef, chicken, pork or seafood along for the ride!

Water	8 cups	2 L
Salt	1/2 tsp.	2 mL
Medium rice stick noodles	9 oz.	250 g
Sesame oil (for flavour)	2 tsp.	10 mL
Brown sugar, packed	2 tbsp.	30 mL
Lime juice	2 tbsp.	30 mL
Soy sauce	2 tbsp.	30 mL
Sweet chili sauce	2 tbsp.	30 mL
Grated lime zest	1 tsp.	5 mL
Dried crushed chilies	1/8 tsp.	0.5 mL

Combine water and salt in large saucepan or Dutch oven. Bring to a boil. Add noodles. Remove from heat. Let stand, covered, for 8 to 10 minutes, until tender but firm. Drain. Return to same pot.

Add sesame oil. Toss. Cover to keep warm.

Combine remaining 6 ingredients in small bowl. Add to noodles. Toss. Makes about 3 1/2 cups (875 mL).

1 cup (250 mL): 155 Calories; 3.6 g Total Fat (1.0 g Mono, 1.1 g Poly, 0.7 g Sat); 0 mg Cholesterol; 29 g Carbohydrate; trace Fibre; 3 g Protein; 763 mg Sodium

Chipotle Perogies

*Sauerkraut and sour cream are all well and good, but we feel that
the potential of the humble perogy has gone unexplored for
far too long. Paired with a creamy chipotle pepper sauce,
this side will add zing to chicken, pork chops or sausage.*

Water	12 cups	3 L
Salt	1/2 tsp.	2 mL
Frozen potato perogies	16	16
Cooking oil	1 tsp.	5 mL
Chopped onion	2/3 cup	150 mL
Chopped roasted red pepper	2/3 cup	150 mL
Finely chopped chipotle pepper in adobo sauce (see Tip, page 49)	1 tsp.	5 mL
Granulated sugar	1/2 tsp.	2 mL
Chili powder	1/4 tsp.	1 mL
Salt	1/8 tsp.	0.5 mL
Pepper	1/8 tsp.	0.5 mL
Ricotta cheese	2/3 cup	150 mL
Grated Asiago cheese	1/4 cup	60 mL

Combine water and salt in Dutch oven or large pot. Bring to a boil.
Add perogies. Boil, uncovered, for about 5 minutes until perogies float
to surface. Drain well. Arrange in single layer in greased 2 quart (2 L)
baking dish. Cover to keep warm.

Heat cooking oil in medium saucepan on medium. Add onion. Cook for
about 5 minutes, stirring occasionally, until softened.

Add next 6 ingredients. Stir. Cook for 10 minutes, stirring occasionally,
to blend flavours. Remove from heat.

Add ricotta cheese. Carefully process with hand blender or in blender until
smooth. Pour over perogies. Toss until coated.

Sprinkle with Asiago cheese. Broil on centre rack in oven for about
5 minutes until cheese is melted and sauce is bubbling. Serves 4.

*1 cup (250 mL): 281 Calories; 10.7 g Total Fat (2.1 g Mono, 0.5 g Poly, 5.3 g Sat);
33 mg Cholesterol; 34 g Carbohydrate; 3 g Fibre; 11 g Protein; 543 mg Sodium*

Pasta & Noodles

Citrus Butter Noodles

Everything's better with butter—margarine just can't compare!
We've countered the richness of the butter with tangy orange and
lemon zest to make a light side for baked chicken, pork or ham.

Water	12 cups	3 L
Salt	1 1/2 tsp.	7 mL
Linguine	8 oz.	225 g
Butter	3 tbsp.	50 mL
Grated lemon zest	1 tsp.	5 mL
Grated orange zest	1 tsp.	5 mL
Ground nutmeg	1/4 tsp.	1 mL
Orange juice	2 tbsp.	30 mL
Lemon juice	1 tbsp.	15 mL
Salt	1/2 tsp.	2 mL
Pepper	1/4 tsp.	1 mL

Combine water and salt in Dutch oven or large pot. Bring to a boil.
Add pasta. Boil, uncovered, for 9 to 11 minutes, stirring occasionally,
until tender but firm. Drain. Return to same pot. Cover to keep warm.

Melt butter in large frying pan on medium. Add next 3 ingredients.
Heat and stir for 1 minute.

Add remaining 4 ingredients. Bring to a boil. Add pasta. Toss until coated.
Makes about 2 1/2 cups (625 mL).

1 cup (250 mL): 461 Calories; 15 g Total Fat (3.6 g Mono, 0.5 g Poly, 9.1 g Sat); 36 mg Cholesterol;
70 g Carbohydrate; 3 g Fibre; 13 g Protein; 569 mg Sodium

 tip Chipotle chili peppers are smoked jalapeño peppers. Be sure to wash
your hands after handling. To store any leftover chipotle chili peppers,
divide into recipe-friendly portions and freeze, with sauce, in airtight
containers for up to one year.

Speedy Summer Shell Salad

Got steak, ribs or burgers on the barbie? Just toss this simple salad together while they grill for the easiest summertime meal imaginable.

Water	8 cups	2 L
Salt	1 tsp.	5 mL
Medium shell pasta	2 cups	500 mL
Chopped fresh spinach, lightly packed	1 cup	250 mL
Chopped fresh tomato	1 cup	250 mL
Ranch dressing	1/4 cup	60 mL

Coarsely ground pepper, sprinkle

Combine water and salt in large saucepan or Dutch oven. Bring to a boil. Add pasta. Boil, uncovered, for 10 to 12 minutes, stirring occasionally, until tender but firm. Drain. Rinse with cold water. Drain well. Transfer to large bowl.

Add next 3 ingredients. Toss.

Sprinkle with pepper. Makes about 4 cups (1 L).

1 cup (250 mL): 518 Calories; 9.6 g Total Fat (trace Mono, 0.1 g Poly, 1.7 g Sat); 4 mg Cholesterol; 92 g Carbohydrate; 5 g Fibre; 17 g Protein; 162 mg Sodium

Pictured on page 53.

Cheesy Pesto Couscous

Here's another quick side that can be made in your microwave. Tangy tomato pesto and Parmesan add flair to couscous. Serve with chicken, pork or fish.

Prepared vegetable broth	1 1/2 cups	375 mL
Couscous	1 cup	250 mL
Grated Parmesan cheese	1/4 cup	60 mL
Sun-dried tomato pesto	2 tsp.	10 mL

Combine broth and couscous in ungreased 1 1/2 quart (1.5 L) casserole. Microwave, covered, on high (100%) for about 3 minutes until couscous is tender and broth is absorbed.

(continued on next page)

Add cheese and pesto. Stir. Makes about 2 1/2 cups (625 mL).

1 cup (250 mL): 345 Calories; 4.4 g Total Fat (1.5 g Mono, 0.4 g Poly, 2.1 g Sat); 8 mg Cholesterol; 61 g Carbohydrate; 3 g Fibre; 14 g Protein; 774 mg Sodium

Nacho Perogies

Jalapeño, cheese and salsa give a nacho twist to traditional perogies.
Serve with ham, sausages or meatloaf.

Water	12 cups	3 L
Salt	1/2 tsp.	2 mL
Frozen potato Cheddar perogies	16	16
Can of diced tomatoes, drained	14 oz.	398 mL
Canned sliced jalapeño pepper chopped (see Tip, below)	2 tsp.	10 mL
Salsa	1 cup	250 mL
Grated Mexican cheese blend	1 cup	250 mL

Combine water and salt in Dutch oven or large pot. Bring to a boil. Add perogies. Boil, uncovered, for about 5 minutes, stirring occasionally, until perogies float to surface. Drain well. Arrange in single layer in greased 2 quart (2 L) baking dish.

Sprinkle tomatoes and jalapeño pepper over perogies. Pour salsa over top. Sprinkle with cheese. Broil on centre rack in oven for about 5 minutes until cheese is melted and bubbling. Serves 4.

1 serving: 304 Calories; 11.0 g Total Fat (0 g Mono, 0 g Poly, 6.7 g Sat); 32 mg Cholesterol; 36 g Carbohydrate; 3 g Fibre; 11 g Protein; 1010 mg Sodium

 tip   Hot peppers contain capsaicin in the seeds and ribs. Removing the seeds and ribs will reduce the heat. Wear rubber gloves when handling hot peppers and avoid touching your eyes. Wash your hands well afterwards.

Feta Lemon Penne Salad

This fresh pasta salad with tender spinach, fresh herbs and bright lemon is a super choice for your next meal of chicken or fish.

Water	8 cups	2 L
Salt	1 tsp.	5 mL
Penne pasta	1 1/2 cups	375 mL
Chopped fresh spinach leaves, lightly packed	2 cups	500 mL
Crumbled feta cheese	1/2 cup	125 mL
Chopped fresh basil	2 tbsp.	30 mL
Grated lemon zest	1 tbsp.	15 mL
Capers (optional)	2 tbsp.	30 mL
Italian dressing	1/4 cup	60 mL

Combine water and salt in large saucepan or Dutch oven. Bring to a boil. Add pasta. Boil, uncovered, for 14 to 16 minutes, stirring occasionally, until tender but firm. Drain. Rinse with cold water. Drain well. Transfer to large bowl.

Add next 5 ingredients. Drizzle with dressing. Toss. Makes about 4 cups (1 L).

1 cup (250 mL): 305 Calories; 15.1 g Total Fat (6.5 g Mono, 3.5 g Poly, 3.6 g Sat); 27 mg Cholesterol; 33 g Carbohydrate; 2 g Fibre; 9 g Protein; 470 mg Sodium

Pictured at right.

1. Feta Lemon Penne Salad, above
2. Speedy Summer Shell Salad, page 50

Props courtesy of: Casa Bugatti
Stokes

Orange Soy Noodles

Say "soy long" to flavourless noodle dishes! We've added an unexpected Asian twist to these sweet and tangy noodles that are a perfect fit for chicken or pork.

Water	8 cups	2 L
Salt	1 tsp.	5 mL
Broad egg noodles	4 cups	1 L
Orange juice	1/3 cup	75 mL
Soy sauce	2 tbsp.	30 mL
Brown sugar, packed	2 tsp.	10 mL
Sesame oil (for flavour)	2 tsp.	10 mL
Grated orange zest	1 tsp.	5 mL
Garlic powder	1/2 tsp.	2 mL
Pepper	1/4 tsp.	1 mL

Combine water and salt in Dutch oven. Bring to a boil. Add noodles. Boil, uncovered, for 10 to 12 minutes, stirring occasionally, until tender but firm. Drain. Return to same pot.

Whisk remaining 7 ingredients in small bowl until smooth. Add to noodles. Toss. Makes about 4 cups (1 L).

1 cup (250 mL): 184 Calories; 2.7 g Total Fat (0.9 g Mono, 0.9 g Poly, 0.3 g Sat); 4 mg Cholesterol; 34 g Carbohydrate; 1 g Fibre; 7 g Protein; 772 mg Sodium

Pictured at left.

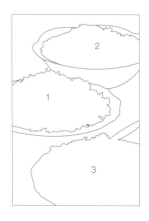

1. Orange Soy Noodles, above
2. Ratatouille Fusilli, page 56
3. Artichoke Pasta, page 57

Props courtesy of: Mikasa Home Store
Pfaltzgraff Canada

Ratatouille Fusilli

So simple, yet so good! Pasta and lots of fresh vegetables are tossed in a tangy
tomato sauce for a fresh, healthy taste. Serve with beef, chicken, pork or fish.

Water	8 cups	2 L
Salt	1 tsp.	5 mL
Fusilli pasta	2 cups	500 mL
Olive (or cooking) oil	1 tsp.	5 mL
Thinly sliced celery	3/4 cup	175 mL
Chopped onion	1/2 cup	125 mL
Garlic clove, minced	1	1
(or 1/4 tsp., 1 mL, powder)		
Can of diced tomatoes (with juice)	14 oz.	398 mL
Large green pepper, cut into	1	1
1 inch (2.5 cm) pieces		
Large red pepper, cut into	1	1
1 inch (2.5 cm) pieces		
Italian seasoning	1 tsp.	5 mL
Pepper	1/4 tsp.	1 mL

Combine water and salt in large saucepan or Dutch oven. Bring to a boil.
Add pasta. Boil, uncovered, for 7 to 9 minutes, stirring occasionally, until
tender but firm. Drain. Return to same pot. Cover to keep warm.

Heat olive oil in large frying pan on medium. Add next 3 ingredients.
Cook for 2 to 4 minutes, stirring often, until celery and onion start to soften.

Add next 5 ingredients. Stir. Bring to a boil. Reduce heat to medium.
Cook, covered, for 5 to 10 minutes until vegetables are tender-crisp.
Add to pasta. Stir. Makes about 6 cups (1.5 L).

1 cup (250 mL): 81 Calories; 1.2 g Total Fat (0.6 g Mono, 0.1 g Poly, 0.2 g Sat); 0 mg Cholesterol;
16 g Carbohydrate; 2 g Fibre; 3 g Protein; 208 mg Sodium

Pictured on page 54.

Artichoke Pasta

We've tossed bow tie pasta with artichokes, olives and sun-dried tomatoes
for a tasty side with all the flavours of Italy. Serve with
grilled beef, chicken, pork or seafood.

Water	8 cups	2 L
Salt	1/2 tsp.	2 mL
Medium bow pasta	2 cups	500 mL
Bacon slices, diced	2	2
Garlic cloves, minced	2	2
(or 1/2 tsp., 2 mL, powder)		
Can of artichoke hearts,	14 oz.	398 mL
drained and chopped		
Sliced black olives	1/3 cup	75 mL
Chopped sun-dried tomatoes in oil	1/4 cup	60 mL
Salt	1/4 tsp.	1 mL
Pepper	1/4 tsp.	1 mL
Olive oil	1 tbsp.	15 mL

Combine water and salt in large saucepan or Dutch oven. Bring to a boil. Add pasta. Boil, uncovered, for 12 to 14 minutes, stirring occasionally, until tender but firm. Drain. Return to same pot. Cover to keep warm.

Heat large frying pan on medium. Add bacon and garlic. Cook for 5 to 8 minutes, stirring occasionally, until bacon is crisp.

Add next 5 ingredients. Cook for about 5 minutes, stirring occasionally, until heated through. Add to pasta. Toss.

Drizzle with olive oil. Stir. Makes about 4 cups (1 L).

1 cup (250 mL): 628 Calories; 15.0 g Total Fat (9.0 g Mono, 1.9 g Poly, 4.5 g Sat); 8 mg Cholesterol; 106 g Carbohydrate; 11 g Fibre; 22 g Protein; 998 mg Sodium

Pictured on page 54.

Pictured on page 54.

Nutty Noodles

This Thai-inspired side has a creamy sauce of peanut, lime and ginger over fresh noodles and crisp vegetables. Perfect for grilled beef, chicken, pork or fish.

Brown sugar, packed	2 tbsp.	30 mL
Lime juice	2 tbsp.	30 mL
Smooth peanut butter	2 tbsp.	30 mL
Soy sauce	2 tbsp.	30 mL
Ground ginger	1/2 tsp.	2 mL
Water	8 cups	2 L
Salt	1 tsp.	5 mL
Fresh, thin Chinese-style egg noodles	8 oz.	225 g
Snow peas, trimmed and halved	1 cup	250 mL
Julienned carrot (see Tip, page 113)	1/2 cup	125 mL

Combine first 5 ingredients in small bowl. Set aside.

Combine water and salt in large saucepan or Dutch oven. Bring to a boil. Add noodles. Boil, uncovered, for 2 minutes, stirring occasionally.

Add snow peas and carrot. Stir. Cook for about 1 minute until vegetables are tender-crisp and noodles are tender but firm. Drain, reserving 2 tbsp. (30 mL) cooking water. Return pasta to same pot. Add reserved cooking water to lime mixture. Stir. Drizzle over pasta mixture. Toss. Makes about 4 cups (1 L).

1 cup (250 mL): 261 Calories; 4.8 g Total Fat (1.2 g Mono, 1.2 g Poly, 0.9 g Sat); 5 mg Cholesterol; 46 g Carbohydrate; 3 g Fibre; 11 g Protein; 802 mg Sodium

Paré Pointer

Boats are the cheapest form of transportation—they run on water.

Creamy Broccoli Rotini

When your hunger's not so teeny, turn to this rotini! This hearty pasta's loaded
with broccoli and cheese for a filling side to chicken, pork and seafood.

Water	8 cups	2 L
Salt	1 tsp.	5 mL
Rotini pasta	2 cups	500 mL
Broccoli florets	2 cups	500 mL
Herb and garlic cream cheese	1/2 cup	125 mL
Milk	1/4 cup	60 mL
Grated Asiago cheese	2 tbsp.	30 mL
Salt, sprinkle		
Pepper, sprinkle		

Combine water and salt in large saucepan or Dutch oven. Bring to a boil.
Add pasta. Boil, uncovered, for 7 minutes, stirring occasionally.

Add broccoli. Cook for 2 to 4 minutes, stirring occasionally, until pasta is
tender but firm and broccoli is tender-crisp. Drain. Transfer to medium
bowl. Cover to keep warm.

Combine cream cheese and milk in same pot. Heat and stir on medium
until smooth. Add pasta mixture. Toss. Transfer to serving bowl.

Sprinkle with remaining 3 ingredients. Makes about 3 cups (750 mL).

1 cup (250 mL): 213 Calories; 11.6 g Total Fat (0.1 g Mono, 0.1 g Poly, 7.2 g Sat);
45 mg Cholesterol; 21 g Carbohydrate; 2 g Fibre; 7 g Protein; 254 mg Sodium

Sweet Potato Hash Browns

Our sweet potato version of hash browns adds a unique
twist to this breakfast—and now dinnertime—favourite.

Olive (or cooking) oil	2 tbsp.	30 mL
Cubed fresh peeled	4 cups	1 L
orange-fleshed sweet potato		
Fresh thyme (or 1/4 tsp., 1 mL, dried)	1 1/2 tsp.	7 mL
Salt	1/4 tsp.	1 mL
Pepper	1/4 tsp.	1 mL
Prepared chicken broth	2 tbsp.	30 mL

Heat olive oil in large frying pan on medium-high. Add sweet potato.
Cook for 5 to 8 minutes, stirring often, until starting to brown on edges.
Reduce heat to medium.

Sprinkle with next 3 ingredients. Stir. Add broth. Cook, covered,
for 5 to 10 minutes, stirring occasionally, until tender. Makes about
3 cups (750 mL).

1 cup (250 mL): 207 Calories; 9.3 g Total Fat (6.7 g Mono, 0.9 g Poly, 1.3 g Sat); 0 mg Cholesterol;
29 g Carbohydrate; 5 g Fibre; 3 g Protein; 307 mg Sodium

Chili Oven Fries

The surprise in these fries is definitely the sweet and spicy seasoning.
For the perfect complementary condiment, serve with
Chipotle Red Pepper Ketchup, page 149.

Cooking oil	3 tbsp.	50 mL
Chili powder	1 tbsp.	15 mL
Ground cinnamon	1 1/2 tsp.	7 mL
Salt	1 1/2 tsp.	7 mL
Unpeeled yellow potatoes	2 1/2 lbs.	1.1 kg
(such as Yukon Gold),		
about 5 medium		

Combine first 4 ingredients in large bowl.

(continued on next page)

Potatoes

Cut potatoes lengthwise into 1/2 inch (12 mm) thick slices. Cut slices lengthwise into 1/2 inch (12 mm) pieces to make fries. Add to spice mixture. Toss until coated. Spread evenly on ungreased baking sheet with sides. Bake in 450°F (230°C) oven for about 40 minutes, turning once, until crisp and tender. Makes about 6 cups (1.5 L).

1 cup (250 mL): 194 Calories; 7.1 g Total Fat (4.1 g Mono, 2.1 g Poly, 0.5 g Sat); 0 mg Cholesterol; 34 g Carbohydrate; 4 g Fibre; 5 g Protein; 598 mg Sodium

---

Spicy Skewered Potatoes

Creamy on the inside with spiced a-peel! Make these ahead of time and grill them alongside your favourite meat for a meal in no time.

Baby potatoes, larger ones cut in half	1 1/2 lbs.	680 g
Bamboo skewers (8 inches, 20 cm, each), soaked in water for 10 minutes	6	6
Olive oil	1 tbsp.	15 mL
Montreal steak spice	2 tsp.	10 mL
Garlic powder	1/8 tsp.	0.5 mL

Pour water into medium saucepan until about 1 inch (2.5 cm) deep. Add potatoes. Cover. Bring to a boil. Reduce heat to medium. Boil gently for 8 to 10 minutes until just tender. Drain. Let stand for about 10 minutes until cool enough to handle.

Thread potatoes onto skewers.

Combine remaining 3 ingredients in small cup. Brush on potatoes. Preheat gas barbecue to medium-high (see Tip, below). Cook potatoes on ungreased grill for about 10 minutes, turning occasionally, until browned. Transfer potatoes from skewers to large bowl. Serves 4.

1 serving: 172 Calories; 3.4 g Total Fat (2.5 g Mono, 0.3 g Poly, 0.5 g Sat); 0 mg Cholesterol; 30 g Carbohydrate; 2 g Fibre; 4 g Protein; 215 mg Sodium

 tip Too cold to barbecue? Use the broiler instead! Your food should cook in about the same length of time—and remember to turn or baste as directed. Set your oven rack so that the food is about 3 to 4 inches (7.5 to 10 cm) away from the top element—for most ovens, this is the top rack.

Spinach-Stuffed Potatoes

Make like Popeye and pack crisp potato shells with delicious and nutritious spinach in a creamy nutmeg-flavoured sauce. It's a very unique and delicious interpretation of the stuffed potato.

Large unpeeled baking potatoes	2	2
Cooking oil	1 tsp.	5 mL
Chopped onion	1/2 cup	125 mL
Garlic cloves, minced (or 1/2 tsp., 2 mL, powder)	2	2
Evaporated milk	1/2 cup	125 mL
Ground nutmeg	1/4 tsp.	1 mL
Salt	1/2 tsp.	2 mL
Pepper	1/4 tsp.	1 mL
Box of frozen chopped spinach, thawed and squeezed dry	10 oz.	300 g
Cooking spray		
Grated Parmesan cheese	1/4 cup	60 mL

Poke several holes randomly with fork into each potato. Microwave, uncovered, on high (100%) for 10 minutes, turning at halftime, until tender. Wrap in tea towel. Let stand for 10 minutes. Unwrap. Let stand for 10 minutes until cool enough to handle. Cut potatoes in half lenthwise. Scoop out pulp, leaving 1/4 inch (6 mm) shell. Mash pulp in medium bowl.

Heat cooking oil in medium frying pan. Add onion and garlic. Cook for 5 to 10 minutes until onion is softened.

Add next 4 ingredients. Heat and stir for about 1 minute until boiling.

Add spinach. Stir. Add to potato. Stir. Spray outside of potato shells with cooking spray. Arrange on baking sheet. Spoon spinach mixture into potato shells. Sprinkle with cheese. Bake in 425°F (220°C) oven for about 20 minutes until heated through and cheese is golden. Makes 4 stuffed potatoes.

1 stuffed potato: 345 Calories; 11.4 g Total Fat (3.8 g Mono, 0.8 g Poly, 6.4 g Sat); 26 mg Cholesterol; 42 g Carbohydrate; 6 g Fibre; 21 g Protein; 961 mg Sodium

Simple Cheddar Scalloped Potatoes

Potatoes + cheesy sauce = dee-lish! (Whoever said math was hard?)
Once you have this simple equation down, try varying the cheese
for a new flavour that you can call your own.

Butter (or hard margarine)	2 tbsp.	30 mL
All-purpose flour	2 tbsp.	30 mL
Milk	1 1/2 cups	375 mL
Grated sharp Cheddar cheese	1 cup	250 mL
Salt	1/4 tsp.	1 mL
Pepper	1/4 tsp.	1 mL
Ground nutmeg, just a pinch		
Peeled baking potatoes, thinly sliced (about 3 medium)	1 1/2 lbs.	680 g
Grated sharp Cheddar cheese	1/2 cup	125 mL
Fine dry bread crumbs	1/4 cup	60 mL

Melt butter in medium saucepan on medium. Add flour. Heat and stir for about 2 minutes until golden brown. Slowly add milk, stirring constantly with whisk, until smooth. Heat and stir until boiling and thickened.

Add next 4 ingredients. Remove from heat. Stir until cheese is melted.

To assemble, layer ingredients in greased 2 quart (2 L) casserole as follows:

1. 1/3 potato slices

2. 1/3 cheese sauce

3. 1/3 potato slices

4. 1/3 cheese sauce

5. Remaining potato slices

6. Remaining cheese sauce

Sprinkle second amount of cheese and bread crumbs over top. Bake, covered, in 350°F (175°C) oven for about 1 hour until potato is tender. Bake, uncovered, for about 10 minutes until golden. Cuts into 6 pieces.

1 piece: 285 Calories; 14.0 g Total Fat (3.9 g Mono, 0.5 g Poly, 8.8 g Sat); 42 mg Cholesterol; 28 g Carbohydrate; 2 g Fibre; 12 g Protein; 378 mg Sodium

Leek And Kale Mashed Potatoes

*Get your starch and veggie meal components done in one
with this cheesy blend of leeks, kale and potatoes. It's a very
flavourful variation of traditional mashed potatoes.*

Peeled potatoes, cut up (about 4 medium)	2 lbs.	900 g
Butter (or hard margarine)	2 tbsp.	30 mL
Chopped kale leaves, lightly packed (see Tip, below)	2 cups	500 mL
Sliced leek (white part only)	2 cups	500 mL
Milk	1 cup	250 mL
Grated Asiago cheese	1/2 cup	125 mL
Salt	1/2 tsp.	2 mL
Pepper	1/4 tsp.	1 mL

Pour water into large saucepan until about 1 inch (2.5 cm) deep.
Add potato. Cover. Bring to a boil. Reduce heat to medium. Boil gently
for 12 to 15 minutes until tender. Drain. Mash. Cover to keep warm.

Melt butter in large frying pan on medium. Add kale and leek. Cook for
about 10 minutes, stirring occasionally, until softened.

Add milk. Stir. Add to potato. Stir.

Add remaining 3 ingredients. Stir. Makes about 5 cups (1.25 L).

*1 cup (250 mL): 300 Calories; 9.2 g Total Fat (1.3 g Mono, 0.4 g Poly, 5.3 g Sat); 24 mg Cholesterol;
48 g Carbohydrate; 5 g Fibre; 9 g Protein; 428 mg Sodium*

 tip   To remove the centre rib from lettuce or kale, fold the leaf in half
along the rib and then cut along the length of the rib.

Potatoes

Sour Cream 'N' Onion Mash

Baked potatoes often get dressed up for dinner with sour cream and chives—but why should they have all the fun? We've added some pizzazz to mashed potatoes for a side that pairs perfectly with beef or chicken.

Peeled potatoes, cut up (about 3 medium)	1 1/2 lbs.	680 g
Butter (or hard margarine)	2 tbsp.	30 mL
Finely chopped onion	3/4 cup	175 mL
Sour cream	3/4 cup	175 mL
Grated sharp Cheddar cheese	1/3 cup	75 mL
Dried chives	2 tsp.	10 mL
Salt	1/2 tsp.	2 mL
Pepper	1/8 tsp.	0.5 mL

Pour water into large saucepan until about 1 inch (2.5 cm) deep. Add potato. Cover. Bring to a boil. Reduce heat to medium. Boil gently for 12 to 15 minutes until tender. Drain. Mash. Cover to keep warm.

Heat butter in small frying pan on medium. Add onion. Cook for 5 to 10 minutes, stirring often, until softened. Add to potato.

Add remaining 5 ingredients. Mash. Makes about 4 1/2 cups (1.1 L).

1 cup (250 mL): 292 Calories; 14.9 g Total Fat (4.1 g Mono, 0.6 g Poly, 9.3 g Sat); 38 mg Cholesterol; 35 g Carbohydrate; 3 g Fibre; 6 g Protein; 375 mg Sodium

SOUR CREAM 'N' ONION CASSEROLE: Spread potato mixture evenly in greased 2 quart (2 L) casserole. Before baking, sprinkle with 3 tbsp. (50 mL) grated sharp Cheddar cheese. Bake, covered, in 350°F (175°C) oven for about 40 minutes until heated through. You can assemble this casserole up to 24 hours in advance and chill until ready to bake.

Butter Sage Potatoes

*Forget the fancy shmancy tonight, this is a case of keeping it simple
and letting the natural flavours shine. This is a quick and
easy side that's made in your microwave.*

Butter (or hard margarine)	1/4 cup	60 mL
Prepared vegetable broth	1/4 cup	60 mL
Dried sage	1/2 tsp.	2 mL
Garlic powder	1/4 tsp.	1 mL
Salt	1/4 tsp.	1 mL
Pepper	1/4 tsp.	1 mL
Cubed unpeeled potato	3 1/2 cups	875 mL
Chopped onion	1/2 cup	125 mL

Combine first 6 ingredients in ungreased 2 quart (2 L) casserole. Microwave, covered, on high (100%) for about 30 seconds until butter is melted. Stir.

Add potato and onion. Toss until coated. Microwave, covered, on high (100%) for 12 to 15 minutes, stirring twice, until tender. Makes about 2 1/2 cups (625 mL).

*1 cup (250 mL): 389 Calories; 18.5 g Total Fat (4.7 g Mono, 0.8 g Poly, 11.6 g Sat);
48 mg Cholesterol; 52 g Carbohydrate; 7 g Fibre; 6 g Protein; 426 mg Sodium*

Slow Cooker Curry Potatoes

*The mild curry flavour of these slow-cooked baby potatoes goes great
with a more intensely flavoured entree of curried pork or chicken.*

Prepared chicken broth	2 cups	500 mL
Brown sugar, packed	1 tsp.	5 mL
Curry powder	1 tsp.	5 mL
Ground ginger	1/2 tsp.	2 mL
Garlic powder	1/4 tsp.	1 mL
Ground cumin	1/4 tsp.	1 mL
Salt	1/4 tsp.	1 mL
Pepper	1/4 tsp.	1 mL
Baby potatoes, cut in half	2 lbs.	900 g

(continued on next page)

Combine first 8 ingredients in 4 quart (4 L) slow cooker.

Add potatoes. Stir. Cook, covered, on Low for 5 to 6 hours or on High for 2 1/2 to 3 hours. Makes about 5 cups (1.25 L).

1 cup (250 mL): 165 Calories; 0.5 g Total Fat (0.2 g Mono, 0.2 g Poly, 0.1 g Sat); 0 mg Cholesterol; 34 g Carbohydrate; 2 g Fibre; 5 g Protein; 722 mg Sodium

---

Grilled Potato Wedges

These crispy-crumbed wedges have a great smoky flavour that pairs perfectly with steaks or burgers.

All-purpose flour	1/2 cup	125 mL
Fine dry bread crumbs	1/2 cup	125 mL
Garlic powder	1 tsp.	5 mL
Seasoned salt	1 tsp.	5 mL
Pepper	1/2 tsp.	2 mL
Large eggs	2	2
Medium unpeeled baking potatoes, cut lengthwise into 1/2 inch (12 mm) wedges	4	4

Cooking spray

Combine first 5 ingredients in large resealable freezer bag.

Whisk eggs in large bowl. Add potato. Toss until coated. Transfer half of potato to flour mixture. Toss until coated. Shake off excess flour mixture. Place, skin-side down, on large baking sheet. Repeat with remaining potato.

Spray potato with cooking spray. Preheat gas barbecue to medium. Arrange wedges on their sides on greased grill. Close lid. Cook for about 12 minutes per side until browned and tender. Serves 8.

1 serving: 94 Calories; 1.3 g Total Fat (0.6 g Mono, 0.2 g Poly, 0.4 g Sat); 47 mg Cholesterol; 18 g Carbohydrate; 2 g Fibre; 4 g Protein; 156 mg Sodium

BAKED POTATO WEDGES: Place coated wedges, skin-side down, on greased baking sheet with sides. Bake in 450°F (230°C) oven for about 30 minutes until tender.

1-2-3 Potato Cakes

There are three types of potatoes in these Cajun-flavoured cakes.
Serve with ham steaks or poached eggs.

Large egg, fork-beaten	1	1
Grated peeled potato	1 cup	250 mL
Grated fresh orange-fleshed sweet potato	1/2 cup	125 mL
Grated fresh yellow-fleshed sweet potato	1/2 cup	125 mL
Fine dry bread crumbs	1/4 cup	60 mL
Sliced green onion	2 tbsp.	30 mL
Cajun seasoning	1 tsp.	5 mL
Pepper	1/2 tsp.	2 mL

Combine all 8 ingredients in large bowl. Form into cakes, using 1/4 cup (60 mL) for each. Arrange in single layer on parchment paper-lined baking sheet with sides. Flatten to 1/8 inch (3 mm) thickness. Bake on centre rack in 400°F (205°C) oven for 15 to 20 minutes until browned. Makes 8 cakes.

1 cake: 62 Calories; 0.9 g Total Fat (0.4 g Mono, 0.2 g Poly, 0.3 g Sat); 23 mg Cholesterol; 12 g Carbohydrate; 1 g Fibre; 2 g Protein; 114 mg Sodium

Grilled Curry Potatoes

These foil packets cook nicely alongside an entree of grilled chicken or pork.

Unpeeled potatoes, cut into 1/4 inch (6 mm) slices (about 4 medium)	2 lbs.	900 g
Cooking oil	1 tbsp.	15 mL
Curry powder	2 tsp.	10 mL
Seasoned salt	1 tsp.	5 mL
Pepper	1/4 tsp.	1 mL

Cut 2 pieces of foil, 12 x 14 inches (30 x 35 cm), each. Spray with cooking spray. Combine all 5 ingredients in large bowl. Spread half of potato mixture on each foil sheet. Fold edges of foil together over potato mixture to enclose. Fold ends to seal completely. Preheat gas barbecue to medium-high. Place packets on ungreased grill. Cook for 20 to 25 minutes, turning at halftime, until potato is tender. Makes about 5 cups (1.25 L).

(continued on next page)

1 cup (250 mL): 150 Calories; 2.8 g Total Fat (1.7 g Mono, 0.8 g Poly, 0.2 g Sat); 0 mg Cholesterol; 32 g Carbohydrate; 4 g Fibre; 5 g Protein; 280 mg Sodium

Pictured on front cover.

BAKED CURRY POTATOES: Spread potato mixture on greased baking sheet with sides. Bake in 450°F (230°C) oven for 25 to 30 minutes until golden and tender.

Pleasing Potato Salad

This justifiably jaunty potato salad is far too good to be relegated to picnic fare alone! Make it your dinner staple whenever you're serving sausage, ham or meatloaf.

Baby potatoes, quartered	1 1/2 lbs.	680 g
Salt	1 tbsp.	15 mL
Sliced green onion	1/2 cup	125 mL
Large hard-cooked eggs, coarsely chopped	2	2
Dry (or alcohol-free) white wine	1/3 cup	75 mL
Olive (or cooking) oil	1/3 cup	75 mL
Chopped fresh parsley	3 tbsp.	50 mL
Dijon mustard (with whole seeds)	1 1/2 tbsp.	25 mL
Liquid honey	1 tbsp.	15 mL
Garlic cloves, minced	3	3
Salt	1 tsp.	5 mL
Pepper, just a pinch		
Chopped fresh parsley, for garnish		

Pour water into large saucepan until about 1 inch (2.5 cm) deep. Add potatoes and salt. Cover. Bring to a boil. Reduce heat to medium. Boil gently for 12 to 15 minutes until tender. Drain. Transfer to large bowl.

Add green onion and egg.

Combine next 8 ingredients in jar with tight-fitting lid. Shake well. Drizzle over potato mixture. Toss until coated.

Garnish with parsley. Serve at room temperature. Makes about 5 cups (1.25 L).

1 cup (250 mL): 304 Calories; 16.7 g Total Fat (11.5 g Mono, 1.5 g Poly, 2.6 g Sat); 74 mg Cholesterol; 30 g Carbohydrate; 2 g Fibre; 6 g Protein; 595 mg Sodium

Golden Asiago Potatoes

Easy, peasy, nice and cheesy! This layered potato dish is filled with the rich flavours of Asiago and rosemary. Serve with roasted chicken, baked ham or roast beef.

Grated Asiago cheese	1/2 cup	125 mL
Garlic butter, melted	2 tbsp.	30 mL
Chopped fresh rosemary	1 tsp.	5 mL
(or 1/4 tsp., 1 mL, dried, crushed)		
Thinly sliced peeled potato	5 cups	1.25 L
Garlic butter, melted	1 tbsp.	15 mL

Combine first 3 ingredients in large bowl.

Add potato. Toss until coated. Brush bottom and side of 9 inch (22 cm) pie plate with second amount of melted garlic butter. Arrange potato in overlapping layers. Bake in 425°F (220°C) oven for about 40 minutes until tender. Run knife around inside edge of pie plate to loosen potato. Invert onto large plate. Cuts into 8 wedges.

1 wedge: 149 Calories; 6.5 g Total Fat (0 g Mono, trace Poly, 3.2 g Sat); 14 mg Cholesterol; 20 g Carbohydrate; 2 g Fibre; 3 g Protein; 114 mg Sodium

Pictured at right.

1. Three-Bean Salad, page 12
2. Asian Noodle Salad, page 40
3. Golden Asiago Potatoes, above

Props courtesy of: Mikasa Home Store
               Stokes

Potatoes

Lemon Potato Peppers

Crisp peppers, soft potatoes, sour cream, tangy lemon... A world
of flavours and textures collide in these flavourful stuffed peppers.

Chopped peeled potato	2 cups	500 mL
Chopped fresh peeled orange-fleshed sweet potato	1 cup	250 mL
Sour cream	1/2 cup	125 mL
Grated lemon zest	2 tsp.	10 mL
Dried rosemary, crushed	1/4 tsp.	1 mL
Dried thyme	1/4 tsp.	1 mL
Salt	1/2 tsp.	2 mL
Pepper	1/4 tsp.	1 mL
Small red peppers, halved lengthwise	2	2
Grated Parmesan cheese	1/4 cup	60 mL

Pour water into large saucepan until about 1 inch (2.5 cm) deep.
Add potato and sweet potato. Cover. Bring to a boil. Reduce heat to
medium. Boil gently for 12 to 15 minutes until tender. Drain. Mash.

Add next 6 ingredients. Stir well.

Spoon potato mixture into red pepper halves. Sprinkle with cheese.
Place on ungreased baking sheet with sides. Bake in 425°F (220°C)
oven for about 30 minutes until heated through and red peppers are
tender-crisp. Makes 4 stuffed peppers.

1 stuffed pepper: 207 Calories; 7.5 g Total Fat (1.5 g Mono, 0.3 g Poly, 4.3 g Sat);
17 mg Cholesterol; 30 g Carbohydrate; 4 g Fibre; 7 g Protein; 454 mg Sodium

Pictured at left.

1. Rosemary Potatoes Au Gratin, page 74
2. Crunchy Potato Balls, page 75
3. Lemon Potato Peppers, above

Props courtesy of: Casa Bugatti
                    Corelle
                    Stokes

Rosemary Potatoes Au Gratin

*A rich, rosemary-infused Parmesan cream sauce coats thinly
sliced potatoes and onions—truly an impressive dish.*

Butter (or hard margarine)	2 tbsp.	30 mL
Garlic clove, minced	1	1
(or 1/4 tsp., 1 mL, powder)		
All-purpose flour	2 tbsp.	30 mL
Milk	1 1/2 cups	375 mL
Grated Parmesan cheese	2 tbsp.	30 mL
Dried rosemary, crushed	1 tsp.	5 mL
Salt	1/2 tsp.	2 mL
Pepper	1/4 tsp.	1 mL
Peeled potatoes, thinly sliced	2 lbs.	900 g
(about 4 medium)		
Thinly sliced onion	1 cup	250 mL
Grated Parmesan cheese	1/4 cup	60 mL

Combine butter and garlic in large saucepan. Cook on medium for
1 to 2 minutes until bubbling. Add flour. Heat and stir for 1 minute.

Slowly add milk, stirring constantly with whisk, until smooth. Heat and stir
until boiling and thickened.

Add next 4 ingredients. Stir.

Put potato and onion into large bowl. Add milk mixture. Toss until coated.
Transfer to greased 2 quart (2 L) casserole.

Sprinkle with second amount of cheese. Bake, covered, in 400°F (205°C)
oven for about 45 minutes until tender. Bake, uncovered, for about
15 minutes until browned. Serves 8.

*1 cup (250 mL): 179 Calories; 5.0 g Total Fat (0.9 g Mono, 0.2 g Poly, 2.9 g Sat); 14 mg Cholesterol;
28 g Carbohydrate; 2 g Fibre; 6 g Protein; 291 mg Sodium*

Pictured on page 72.

Crunchy Potato Balls

Got tots? Serve them taters—with way more flavour and way less fat than frozen potato puffs. Adults won't be able to resist them either! Serve with hot dogs or hamburgers.

Peeled potatoes, cut up (about 2 medium)	1 lb.	454 g
Large egg, fork-beaten	1	1
Grated Swiss cheese	1/2 cup	125 mL
Mayonnaise	2 tbsp.	30 mL
Finely chopped green onion	1 tbsp.	15 mL
Fine dry bread crumbs	3/4 cup	175 mL
Seasoned salt	1/2 tsp.	2 mL

Cooking spray

Pour water into medium saucepan until about 1 inch (2.5 cm) deep. Add potato. Cover. Bring to a boil. Reduce heat to medium. Boil gently for 12 to 15 minutes until tender. Drain. Mash. Let stand until cool enough to handle.

Combine next 4 ingredients in large bowl. Add potato. Stir well. Roll into 1 inch (2.5 cm) balls.

Combine bread crumbs and seasoned salt in large shallow dish. Press and roll balls in crumb mixture until coated. Arrange on greased baking sheet with sides.

Spray with cooking spray. Bake in 350°F (175°C) oven for about 30 minutes until golden. Serves 4.

1 serving: 301 Calories; 11.9 g Total Fat (1.0 g Mono, 0.5 g Poly, 3.9 g Sat); 62 mg Cholesterol; 38 g Carbohydrate; 3 g Fibre; 10 g Protein; 445 mg Sodium

Pictured on page 72.

Spicy Peanut Sweet Potatoes

A mildly spicy peanut sauce coats tender sweet potato and cauliflower in this simple side that's great for serving with chicken or pork.

Cooking oil	1 tsp.	5 mL
Chopped onion	1 cup	250 mL
Garlic cloves, minced	2	2
(or 1/2 tsp., 2 mL, powder)		
Finely grated gingerroot	1 tsp.	5 mL
Prepared vegetable broth	1 1/2 cups	375 mL
Thai peanut sauce	2 tbsp.	30 mL
Cubed fresh peeled yellow-fleshed	3 cups	750 mL
sweet potato		
Cauliflower florets	1 1/2 cups	375 mL

Heat cooking oil in large frying pan on medium. Add onion. Cook for 5 to 10 minutes, stirring occasionally, until softened.

Add garlic and ginger. Heat and stir for about 1 minute until fragrant.

Add broth and peanut sauce. Stir. Bring to a boil. Add sweet potato and cauliflower. Stir. Cook, covered, for 15 to 18 minutes, stirring occasionally, until sweet potato and cauliflower are tender. Makes about 3 cups (750 mL).

1 cup (250 mL): 183 Calories; 3.9 g Total Fat (0.9 g Mono, 0.6 g Poly, 0.6 g Sat); 0 mg Cholesterol; 34 g Carbohydrate; 6 g Fibre; 5 g Protein; 472 mg Sodium

Sweet Potato Mash

Blah side dishes have met their mash with this creamy mixed potato blend. Great with baked ham or chicken.

Peeled potatoes, cut up (about 4 medium)	2 lbs.	900 g
Can of sweet potatoes, drained and chopped	19 oz.	540 mL
Milk	1/2 cup	125 mL
Butter (or hard margarine)	2 tbsp.	30 mL
Chopped fresh parsley, for garnish		

(continued on next page)

Pour water into large saucepan until about 1 inch (2.5 cm) deep. Add potato. Cover. Bring to a boil. Reduce heat to medium. Boil gently for 10 to 12 minutes until almost tender.

Add sweet potato. Cover. Boil gently for about 2 minutes until potato is tender. Drain. Mash.

Add milk and butter. Stir well. Transfer to serving bowl.

Garnish with parsley. Makes about 6 cups (1.5 L).

1 cup (250 mL): 270 Calories; 4.4 g Total Fat (1.1 g Mono, 0.3 g Poly, 2.6 g Sat); 11 mg Cholesterol; 54 g Carbohydrate; 5 g Fibre; 5 g Protein; 80 mg Sodium

Warm Roasted Potato Salad

A truly decadent potato salad! With rich, roasted potatoes and red peppers, smoky bacon and spicy Cajun seasoning, this is one side that just might upstage your main course. Goes well with most entrees.

Baby potatoes, quartered	2 lbs.	900 g
Olive oil	1 tbsp.	15 mL
Cajun seasoning	2 tsp.	10 mL
Large red pepper, halved lengthwise	1	1
Mayonnaise	1/2 cup	125 mL
Sour cream	1/2 cup	125 mL
Sliced green onion	1/4 cup	60 mL
Bacon slices, cooked crisp and crumbled	4	4

Put first 3 ingredients into large bowl. Toss until coated. Arrange in single layer on ungreased baking sheet with sides.

Place red pepper, cut-side down, in pie plate. Place on top rack in oven. Place potatoes on bottom rack in oven. Bake at 400°F (205°C) for about 30 minutes until potatoes and red pepper are tender. Transfer red pepper to small bowl. Cover with plastic wrap. Let sweat for 15 minutes until cool enough to handle. Remove and discard skins. Chop.

Combine next 3 ingredients in large bowl. Add bacon, potatoes and red pepper. Stir. Makes about 4 cups (1 L).

1 cup (250 mL): 532 Calories; 33.2 g Total Fat (16.5 g Mono, 6.5 g Poly, 8.1 g Sat); 35 mg Cholesterol; 48 g Carbohydrate; 3 g Fibre; 9 g Protein; 671 mg Sodium

Double-Orange Sweet Potatoes

What you see is what you get! Bright orange sweet potatoes are flavoured with aromatic orange zest and the sweet tartness of orange marmalade.

Chopped fresh peeled orange-fleshed sweet potato	4 cups	1 L
Butter (or hard margarine)	2 tbsp.	30 mL
Orange marmalade	2 tbsp.	30 mL
Grated orange zest	1/2 tsp.	2 mL
Salt	1/8 tsp.	0.5 mL

Pour water into large saucepan until about 1 inch (2.5 cm) deep. Add sweet potato. Cover. Bring to a boil. Reduce heat to medium. Boil gently for 12 to 15 minutes until tender. Drain. Mash.

Add remaining 4 ingredients. Stir until butter is melted. Makes about 3 cups (750 mL).

1 cup (250 mL): 225 Calories; 7.8 g Total Fat (2.0 g Mono, 0.4 g Poly, 4.9 g Sat); 20 mg Cholesterol; 38 g Carbohydrate; 5 g Fibre; 3 g Protein; 208 mg Sodium

Perfect Potatoes

The perfect potatoes need not take forever being boiled or baked, but can be snappily made in the microwave. Serve with chicken, beef, pork or fish.

Baby potatoes, cut in half	1 1/2 lbs.	680 g
Water	1/4 cup	60 mL
Garlic butter, melted	2 tbsp.	30 mL
Finely chopped green onion	2 tbsp.	30 mL
Montreal steak spice	1 tsp.	5 mL

Put potatoes and water into large microwave-safe bowl. Microwave, covered, on high (100%) for about 10 minutes, stirring occasionally, until potatoes are tender. Drain.

Drizzle with melted garlic butter. Sprinkle with green onion and steak spice. Toss. Serves 4.

1 serving: 192 Calories; 5.5 g Total Fat (0 g Mono, 0 g Poly, 2.5 g Sat); 10 mg Cholesterol; 30 g Carbohydrate; 2 g Fibre; 4 g Protein; 188 mg Sodium

Pictured on page 89.

Potatoes

Cajun Potatoes

These pepped-up potatoes pack a punch when paired with beef, chicken or pork.

Cooking oil	2 tbsp.	30 mL
Diced peeled potato	6 cups	1.5 L
Chopped onion	1 1/2 cups	375 mL
Prepared vegetable broth	1 cup	250 mL
Cajun seasoning	4 tsp.	20 mL
Garlic cloves, minced	2	2
(or 1/2 tsp., 2 mL, powder)		

Heat cooking oil in large frying pan on medium-high. Add potato. Cook for 5 to 10 minutes, stirring often, until browned. Reduce heat to medium.

Add remaining 4 ingredients. Stir. Cook, covered, for 10 to 15 minutes, stirring often, until potato is tender. Makes about 5 cups (1.25 L).

1 cup (250 mL): 237 Calories; 6.0 g Total Fat (3.2 g Mono, 1.7 g Poly, 0.5 g Sat); 0 mg Cholesterol; 44 g Carbohydrate; 4 g Fibre; 4 g Protein; 535 mg Sodium

Savoury Potato Puff

The texture may be fluffy, but this creamy casserole is no lightweight when it comes to flavour! Take it to your next potluck and just wait for the rave reviews.

Peeled baking potatoes, cut up	2 lbs.	900 g
(about 4 medium)		
Large egg	1	1
Can of condensed cream of celery soup	10 oz.	284 mL
Grated sharp Cheddar cheese	1 1/2 cups	375 mL

Pour water into large saucepan until about 1 inch (2.5 cm) deep. Add potato. Cover. Bring to a boil. Reduce heat to medium. Boil gently for 12 to 15 minutes until tender. Drain. Mash.

Add egg and soup. Beat until light and smooth. Add cheese. Stir. Transfer to greased 9 x 9 inch (22 x 22 cm) pan. Spread evenly. Bake in 350°F (175°C) oven for about 45 minutes until edges are golden. Makes about 7 cups (1.75 L).

1 cup (250 mL): 253 Calories; 10.9 g Total Fat (2.6 g Mono, 0.3 g Poly, 5.9 g Sat); 54 mg Cholesterol; 30 g Carbohydrate; 3 g Fibre; 9 g Protein; 451 mg Sodium

Dilly Quinoa

Dill adds a familiar flavour to the interesting texture of quinoa.
Serve with chicken or fish.

Chopped onion	1/2 cup	125 mL
Butter (or hard margarine)	1 tbsp.	15 mL
Garlic clove, minced	1	1
(or 1/4 tsp., 1 mL, powder)		
Dried dillweed	1 tsp.	5 mL
Prepared chicken broth	1 1/2 cups	375 mL
Quinoa, rinsed and drained	1 cup	250 mL

Combine first 4 ingredients in large microwave-safe bowl. Microwave, covered, on high (100%) for about 5 minutes, stirring occasionally, until onion is softened.

Add broth and quinoa. Stir. Microwave, covered, on high (100%) for about 2 minutes until boiling. Microwave, covered, on medium (50%) for about 15 minutes until quinoa is tender. Makes about 2 1/2 cups (625 mL).

1 cup (250 mL): 334 Calories; 9.4 g Total Fat (2.6 g Mono, 1.9 g Poly, 3.5 g Sat); 12 mg Cholesterol; 51 g Carbohydrate; 5 g Fibre; 12 g Protein; 514 mg Sodium

Creamy Polenta

Polenta sounds gourmet, and this creamy cornmeal dish is sure to impress
your guests, but only you need to know that it's only got four ingredients—and
cooks in under 10 minutes! Pair with ham steaks or roasted eggplant.

Prepared chicken broth	2 cups	500 mL
Yellow cornmeal	1/2 cup	125 mL
Butter (or hard margarine)	1 tbsp.	15 mL
Herb and garlic cream cheese	1/4 cup	60 mL

Measure broth into large saucepan. Bring to a boil. Slowly add cornmeal, stirring constantly. Reduce heat to medium. Add butter. Cook, uncovered, for about 5 minutes, stirring occasionally, until thickened.

Add cream cheese. Stir until smooth. Makes about 5 cups (1.25 L).

1 cup (250 mL): 114 Calories; 5.9 g Total Fat (0.9 g Mono, 9.3 g Poly, 3.4 g Sat); 18 mg Cholesterol; 11 g Carbohydrate; 1 g Fibre; 4 g Protein; 381 mg Sodium

Barley Vermicelli Pilaf

Remember those boxed rice and pasta dishes? We've done this classic combo one better by replacing the rice with healthy and delicious barley. Kids and nostalgic adults alike will enjoy the simple, savoury flavours.

Cooking oil	1 tbsp.	15 mL
Diced red pepper	1 cup	250 mL
Diced onion	1/2 cup	125 mL
Finely diced carrot	1/2 cup	125 mL
Garlic cloves, minced (or 1/2 tsp., 2 mL, powder)	2	2
Prepared chicken broth	2 3/4 cups	675 mL
Pearl barley	1 cup	250 mL
Basil pesto	1 tsp.	5 mL
Salt	1/4 tsp.	1 mL
Pepper	1/4 tsp.	1 mL
Broken up vermicelli (1 inch, 2.5 cm, pieces)	1/2 cup	125 mL

Chopped fresh parsley, for garnish

Heat cooking oil in medium saucepan on medium. Add next 4 ingredients. Cook, uncovered, for about 10 minutes, stirring occasionally, until onion is softened.

Add next 5 ingredients. Stir. Bring to a boil. Reduce heat to medium-low. Cook, covered, for 20 minutes.

Add pasta. Stir. Cook, covered, for about 10 minutes until pasta is tender and liquid is absorbed.

Garnish with parsley. Makes about 4 1/4 cups (1 L).

1 cup (250 mL): 298 Calories; 5.4 g Total Fat (2.4 g Mono, 1.5 g Poly, 0.7 g Sat); trace Cholesterol; 54 g Carbohydrate; 5 g Fibre; 10 g Protein; 667 mg Sodium

Asian Rice Salad

Keep your menu current—or currant, with this sweet-and-sour rice dish.
Distinct Asian flavours make this a great choice for an ethnic-themed dinner.

Cooking oil	2 tsp.	10 mL
Currants	1/2 cup	125 mL
Finely chopped celery	1/2 cup	125 mL
Finely chopped onion	1/2 cup	125 mL
Grated carrot	1/2 cup	125 mL
Garlic cloves, minced	2	2
(or 1/2 tsp., 2 mL, powder)		
Finely grated gingerroot	2 tsp.	10 mL
(or 1/2 tsp., 2 mL, ground ginger)		
Dried crushed chilies	1/2 tsp.	2 mL
Rice vinegar	3 tbsp.	50 mL
Soy sauce	2 tbsp.	30 mL
Brown sugar, packed	2 tsp.	10 mL
Sesame oil (for flavour)	1 tsp.	5 mL
Cold cooked long grain brown rice	3 cups	750 mL
(about 1 cup, 250 mL, uncooked),		
see Tip, page 85		
Thinly sliced green onion	2 tbsp.	30 mL
Thinly sliced green onion (optional)	2 tbsp.	30 mL
Sliced almonds, toasted	1 tbsp.	15 mL
(see Tip, page 128), optional		
Sesame seeds, toasted	1 tsp.	5 mL
(see Tip, page 128), optional		

Heat cooking oil in medium frying pan on medium. Add next 7 ingredients. Cook for 5 to 10 minutes, stirring occasionally, until onion is softened. Remove from heat.

Add next 4 ingredients. Stir well.

Put rice into large bowl. Add currant mixture and first amount of green onion. Toss. Chill, covered, for 1 to 2 hours until cold.

Sprinkle with remaining 3 ingredients. Makes about 4 cups (1 L).

1 cup (250 mL): 235 Calories; 4.9 g Total Fat (2.3 g Mono, 1.7 g Poly, 0.6 g Sat); 0 mg Cholesterol; 43 g Carbohydrate; 4 g Fibre; 5 g Protein; 689 mg Sodium

Beet Risotto

Sweet beets add flavour and colour to this pretty dish.
Serve with chicken, pork or seafood.

Prepared chicken broth	3 1/2 cups	875 mL
Reserved liquid from sliced beets	1/2 cup	125 mL
Cooking oil	2 tsp.	10 mL
Arborio rice	1 cup	250 mL
Dry (or alcohol-free) white wine	1/2 cup	125 mL
Can of sliced beets, drained and liquid reserved, diced (see Tip, page 117)	14 oz.	398 mL
Grated Parmesan cheese	2 tbsp.	30 mL

Combine broth and reserved beet liquid in medium saucepan. Bring to a boil. Reduce heat to low. Cover to keep hot.

Heat cooking oil in large saucepan on medium. Add rice. Stir until coated. Add wine. Heat and stir until wine is absorbed. Add 1/2 cup (125 mL) broth mixture (see Note). Heat and stir until almost absorbed. Repeat with remaining broth mixture, 1/2 cup (125 mL) at a time, until broth mixture is absorbed and rice is tender.

Add beets. Cook and stir until heated through.

Sprinkle with cheese. Makes about 4 cups (1 L).

1 cup (250 mL): 203 Calories; 4.5 g Total Fat (2.1 g Mono, 1.0 g Poly, 1.1 g Sat); 2 mg Cholesterol; 27 g Carbohydrate; 1 g Fibre; 8 g Protein; 238 mg Sodium

Note: Most soup ladles hold 4 to 6 oz. (114 to 170 mL) and can be used to add the broth to the rice during cooking.

Paré Pointer

When burgers want to dance, they attend a meatball.

Vegetable Quinoa

This easy, healthy side dish goes great with grilled fish or chicken.

Cooking oil	1 tsp.	5 mL
Chopped green pepper	1/2 cup	125 mL
Chopped onion	1/2 cup	125 mL
Finely chopped celery	1/2 cup	125 mL
Finely chopped carrot	1/4 cup	60 mL
Vegetable cocktail juice	1 1/4 cups	300 mL
Water	3/4 cup	175 mL
Salt	1/4 tsp.	1 mL
Quinoa, rinsed and drained	1 cup	250 mL
Dried dillweed	1/2 tsp.	2 mL
Pepper	1/4 tsp.	1 mL

Heat cooking oil in medium saucepan on medium. Add next 4 ingredients. Cook for about 5 minutes, stirring occasionally, until onion is softened.

Add next 3 ingredients. Stir. Bring to a boil. Add quinoa. Stir. Reduce heat to medium-low. Simmer, covered, for about 25 minutes, without stirring, until quinoa is tender and liquid is absorbed. Fluff with fork.

Add dill and pepper. Stir. Makes about 4 cups (1 L).

1 cup (250 mL): 201 Calories; 3.8 g Total Fat (1.3 g Mono, 1.4 g Poly, 0.4 g Sat); 0 mg Cholesterol; 37 g Carbohydrate; 4 g Fibre; 7 g Protein; 378 mg Sodium

Gingery-Sweet Quinoa

When you think of cooked grains, do you picture plain oatmeal? Change your perception of what a grain dish can be with the intriguing texture of quinoa and the tangy sweetness of cranberries and ginger.

Prepared chicken broth	2 cups	500 mL
Salt, just a pinch		
Quinoa, rinsed and drained	1 cup	250 mL
Dried cherries (or cranberries), chopped	1/4 cup	60 mL
Chopped crystallized ginger	2 tbsp.	30 mL

(continued on next page)

Rice & Grains

Combine broth and salt in medium saucepan. Bring to a boil. Add remaining 3 ingredients. Stir. Reduce heat to medium-low. Simmer, covered, for about 30 minutes, without stirring, until quinoa is tender and broth is absorbed. Fluff with fork. Makes about 3 cups (750 mL).

1 cup (250 mL): 287 Calories; 4.2 g Total Fat (1.3 g Mono, 1.5 g Poly, 0.6 g Sat); 0 mg Cholesterol; 51 g Carbohydrate; 6 g Fibre; 11 g Protein; 532 mg Sodium

Salsa Rice Salad

Get ready to salsa! This easy salad has lots of colour and fresh Mexican flavour —truly something to dance about! Goes great with chicken, pork or fish.

Cold cooked long grain white rice (about 1 1/3 cup, 325 mL, uncooked), see Tip, below	4 cups	1 L
Chopped green onion	1/4 cup	60 mL
Chopped fresh cilantro or parsley	2 tbsp.	30 mL
Lime juice	2 tbsp.	30 mL
Olive (or cooking) oil	2 tbsp.	30 mL
Ground cumin	1/2 tsp.	2 mL
Cayenne pepper	1/8 tsp.	0.5 mL
Salsa	1/2 cup	125 mL

Combine rice and green onion in large bowl.

Whisk next 5 ingredients in small bowl. Add salsa. Stir. Drizzle over rice mixture. Toss gently. Makes about 4 cups (1 L).

1 cup (250 mL): 281 Calories; 7.3 g Total Fat (5.1 g Mono, 0.7 g Poly, 1.0 g Sat); 0 mg Cholesterol; 48 g Carbohydrate; 1 g Fibre; 5 g Protein; 129 mg Sodium

 tip   If your cold rice is clumping together, wet your hands slightly and break the clumps apart with your fingers—this will prevent the rice from sticking to your hands.

Bulgur Chickpea Curry

Chickpea curries are a tasty staple at Indo-Asian restaurants.
We've added nutty bulgur for a one-two punch of nutritious grains
and legumes. Serve with pork or lamb stew, fish or grilled chicken.

Prepared vegetable broth	1 1/4 cups	300 mL
Curry powder	1 tsp.	5 mL
Ground cinnamon	1/4 tsp.	1 mL
Ground cumin	1/4 tsp.	1 mL
Bulgur	3/4 cup	175 mL
Cooking oil	1 tsp.	5 mL
Chopped onion	1 cup	250 mL
Garlic cloves, minced	2	2
(or 1/2 tsp., 2 mL, powder)		
Can of chickpeas (garbanzo beans), rinsed and drained	19 oz.	540 mL
Finely chopped red pepper	1 cup	250 mL
Salt	1/2 tsp.	2 mL
Pepper	1/4 tsp.	1 mL

Combine first 4 ingredients in small saucepan. Bring to a boil.

Add bulgur. Stir. Reduce heat to medium-low. Simmer, covered, for 25 minutes, without stirring. Remove from heat. Let stand, covered, for about 5 minutes until bulgur is tender and liquid is absorbed. Fluff with fork.

Heat cooking oil in medium frying pan on medium. Add onion and garlic. Cook for 5 to 10 minutes, stirring occasionally, until onion is softened.

Add remaining 4 ingredients. Heat and stir for 2 to 4 minutes until red pepper is tender-crisp. Transfer to medium bowl. Add bulgur. Stir. Makes about 5 cups (1.25 L).

1 cup (250 mL): 283 Calories; 4.2 g Total Fat (1.2 g Mono, 1.7 g Poly, 0.4 g Sat); 0 mg Cholesterol; 51 g Carbohydrate; 8 g Fibre; 13 g Protein; 740 mg Sodium

Pictured on page 18.

Tex-Mex Bulgur Salad

Get all the energy you'll need to ride off into the sunset
with this fresh mix of veggies and grains. Serve up with
a big grilled steak for some authentic cowboy cookin'.

Water	1 cup	250 mL
Tomato juice	1/2 cup	125 mL
Ground cumin	2 tsp.	10 mL
Salt	1/2 tsp.	2 mL
Bulgur	1 cup	250 mL
Frozen kernel corn, thawed	2 cups	500 mL
Diced English cucumber (with peel)	1 cup	250 mL
Diced green pepper	1 cup	250 mL
Diced Roma (plum) tomato	1 cup	250 mL
Finely diced red onion	1/2 cup	125 mL
Olive oil	1/4 cup	60 mL
Red wine vinegar	2 tbsp.	30 mL
Garlic clove, minced	1	1
(or 1/4 tsp., 1 mL, powder)		
Chopped fresh cilantro or parsley	1/4 cup	60 mL

Combine first 4 ingredients in small saucepan. Bring to a boil. Add bulgur. Stir. Remove from heat. Let stand, covered, for about 30 minutes until liquid is absorbed. Fluff with fork. Transfer to large bowl. Cool.

Add next 5 ingredients. Toss.

Whisk next 3 ingredients in small bowl. Add cilantro. Stir. Drizzle over bulgur mixture. Toss. Makes about 4 cups (1 L).

1 cup (250 mL): 351 Calories; 15.0 g Total Fat (10.2 g Mono, 1.7 g Poly, 2.1 g Sat); 0 mg Cholesterol; 52 g Carbohydrate; 8 g Fibre; 8 g Protein; 420 mg Sodium

Pictured on page 89.

Grilled Polenta

The southwestern flavours of chili and cheese are terrific in cornbread—so why not polenta? This firm version of the Italian staple gets nicely browned and crispy on the grill. Serve with barbecued ribs or sausages.

Prepared chicken broth	4 cups	1 L
Chili powder	1/2 tsp.	2 mL
Ground cumin	1/2 tsp	2 mL
Yellow cornmeal	1 1/2 cups	375 mL
Grated Mexican cheese blend	1 cup	250 mL
Olive (or cooking) oil	1 tbsp.	15 mL

Combine first 3 ingredients in large saucepan. Bring to a boil. Reduce heat to medium. Slowly add cornmeal, stirring constantly. Heat and stir for about 10 minutes until mixture is thick and pulls away from side of pan.

Add cheese. Stir. Spread evenly in 9 x 9 inch (22 x 22 cm) pan, lined with greased foil. Let stand for 20 minutes. Chill for about 1 hour until set. Remove from pan. Cut into 4 squares. Cut each square in half diagonally.

Brush pieces with olive oil (see Note). Preheat gas barbecue to medium. Cook polenta on well-greased grill for 5 to 7 minutes per side until grill marks appear and polenta is heated through. Makes 8 triangles.

1 triangle: 185 Calories; 7.4 g Total Fat (1.7 g Mono, 0.5 g Poly, 3.5 g Sat); 13 mg Cholesterol; 21 g Carbohydrate; 1 g Fibre; 8 g Protein; 491 mg Sodium

Note: If you're not serving all the polenta right away, grill only the amount you need. Wrap or store extra triangles in an airtight container in the refrigerator for up to 1 week and grill as needed.

1. Tex-Mex Bulgur Salad, page 87
2. Black-Eyed Peas, page 21
3. Perfect Potatoes, page 78

Rice & Grains

Cranberry Wild Rice

Firm grains of wild rice are tossed with tangy cranberries and lots of fresh herbs for a great side to serve with burgers, steaks or grilled pork chops.

Cooking oil	1 tsp.	5 mL
Sliced fresh white mushrooms	2 cups	500 mL
Chopped onion	1 cup	250 mL
Garlic clove, minced	1	1
(or 1/4 tsp., 1 mL, powder)		
Prepared chicken broth	2 1/2 cups	625 mL
Wild rice	1 cup	250 mL
Dried cranberries	1/2 cup	125 mL
Chopped fresh parsley	2 tbsp.	30 mL
Chopped fresh basil	1 tbsp.	15 mL
Chopped fresh thyme	1 tsp.	5 mL

Heat cooking oil in large saucepan on medium. Add next 3 ingredients. Cook, uncovered, for about 10 minutes, stirring occasionally, until mushrooms and onion are softened.

Add broth and rice. Bring to a boil. Reduce heat to medium-low. Simmer, covered, for about 75 minutes, without stirring, until rice is tender.

Add remaining 4 ingredients. Stir. Makes about 4 cups (1 L).

1 cup (250 mL): 268 Calories; 2.9 g Total Fat (1.2 g Mono, 1.0 g Poly, 0.5 g Sat); 0 mg Cholesterol; 53 g Carbohydrate; 5 g Fibre; 11 g Protein; 494 mg Sodium

1. Mushroom Barsotto, page 92
2. Wild Rice Squares, page 93
3. Creole Rice Patties, page 94

Props courtesy of: Mikasa Home Store
Pfaltzgraff Canada

Mushroom Barsotto

Everyone knows about rice risotto, but barley can also be used to make this rich and creamy dish. Hearty flavours make this a great side for roast beef or pork. For best results, make the beer a honey brown or amber ale.

Olive oil	1 tbsp.	15 mL
Chopped portobello mushrooms	5 cups	1.25 L
(about 12 oz., 340 g)		
Prepared vegetable broth	4 cups	1 L
Water	2 cups	500 mL
Olive oil	1 tbsp.	15 mL
Chopped onion	1 cup	250 mL
Pearl barley	1 cup	250 mL
Dark (or alcohol-free) beer	3/4 cup	175 mL
Grated Asiago cheese	1/3 cup	75 mL
Pepper	1/2 tsp.	2 mL

Heat first amount of olive oil in large frying pan on medium-high. Add mushrooms. Cook for 5 to 10 minutes, stirring occasionally, until mushrooms are starting to brown and liquid is evaporated. Remove from heat. Set aside.

Combine broth and water in medium saucepan. Bring to a boil. Reduce heat to low. Cover to keep hot.

Heat second amount of olive oil in large saucepan on medium. Add onion. Cook for about 10 minutes, stirring occasionally, until starting to soften.

Add barley. Heat and stir until coated. Add beer. Heat and stir until liquid is absorbed. Add 1/2 cup (125 mL) broth mixture (see Note). Heat and stir until almost absorbed. Repeat with remaining broth mixture, adding 1/2 cup (125 mL) at a time, until broth mixture is absorbed and barley is tender. Add mushrooms. Cook and stir until heated through.

Add cheese and pepper. Stir. Makes about 5 cups (1.25 L).

1 cup (250 mL): 276 Calories; 8.3 g Total Fat (4.0 g Mono, 0.7 g Poly, 2.1 g Sat); 6 mg Cholesterol; 42 g Carbohydrate; 8 g Fibre; 8 g Protein; 830 mg Sodium

Pictured on page 90.

Note: Most soup ladles hold 4 to 6 oz. (114 to 170 mL) and can be used to add the broth to the barley during cooking.

Wild Rice Squares

Is being square a bad thing? Not for a side dish of nutty wild rice flavoured with Swiss cheese and buttermilk. Serve with roast chicken, pork or salmon.

Water	1 1/2 cups	375 mL
Salt	1/4 tsp.	1 mL
Wild rice	1/2 cup	125 mL
Cooking oil	1 tsp.	5 mL
Thinly sliced fresh white mushrooms	1 cup	250 mL
Chopped onion	1/2 cup	125 mL
Large eggs, fork-beaten	3	3
All-purpose flour	1/2 cup	125 mL
Buttermilk (or soured milk, see Tip, page 31)	1/2 cup	125 mL
Grated Swiss cheese	1 cup	250 mL
Chopped fresh parsley	1 tbsp.	15 mL
(or 3/4 tsp., 4 mL, flakes)		
Salt	1/2 tsp.	2 mL
Pepper	1/2 tsp.	2 mL
Chopped fresh thyme	1/4 tsp.	1 mL
(or dried, just a pinch)		

Combine water and salt in medium saucepan. Bring to a boil. Add rice. Stir. Reduce heat to medium-low. Simmer, covered, for about 75 minutes, without stirring, until rice is tender. Drain any excess water. Rinse under cold water until cool. Drain well. Transfer to large bowl.

Heat cooking oil in large frying pan on medium. Add mushrooms and onion. Cook for about 10 minutes, stirring occasionally, until lightly browned. Add to rice.

Whisk next 3 ingredients in medium bowl. Add remaining 5 ingredients. Mix well. Add to rice mixture. Stir. Transfer to greased 9 x 9 inch (22 x 22 cm) pan. Bake in 350°F (175°C) oven for about 25 minutes until wooden pick inserted in centre comes out clean. Let stand on wire rack for 5 minutes. Cuts into 16 squares.

1 square: 82 Calories; 3.3 g Total Fat (1.1 g Mono, 0.4 g Poly, 1.6 g Sat); 41 mg Cholesterol; 9 g Carbohydrate; 1 g Fibre; 5 g Protein; 143 mg Sodium

Pictured on page 90.

Creole Rice Patties

*Plain white rice gets all dressed up for Mardi Gras with
hot sauce and colourful vegetable bits, then is shaped into patties
and fried to a crispy golden brown. Get the party started by pairing
them with a main course of steak, grilled chicken or pork chops.*

Water	2 cups	500 mL
Celery salt	1/2 tsp.	2 mL
Long grain white rice	1 cup	250 mL
Large egg, fork-beaten	1	1
All-purpose flour	1/4 cup	60 mL
Finely chopped green pepper	1/4 cup	60 mL
Finely chopped red pepper	1/4 cup	60 mL
Grated onion	1/4 cup	60 mL
Dried basil	1/2 tsp.	2 mL
Louisiana hot sauce	1/2 tsp.	2 mL
Salt	1/2 tsp.	2 mL
Cooking oil	2 tbsp.	30 mL

Chopped fresh basil, for garnish

Combine water and celery salt in medium saucepan. Bring to a boil. Add rice.
Stir. Reduce heat to medium-low. Simmer, covered, for 15 minutes, without
stirring. Remove from heat. Let stand, covered, for about 5 minutes until
rice is tender and liquid is absorbed. Fluff with fork. Spread on ungreased
baking sheet with sides. Let stand for about 5 minutes until cool.

Combine next 8 ingredients in large bowl. Add rice. Mix well. Shape into
twelve 2 1/2 inch (6.4 cm) diameter patties, using 1/4 cup (60 mL) for
each (see Note).

Heat 1 tbsp. (15 mL) cooking oil in large frying pan on medium. Cook
6 patties, partially covered, for 2 to 4 minutes per side until browned
and heated through. Repeat with remaining cooking oil and patties.

Garnish with basil. Makes 12 patties.

*1 patty: 100 Calories; 2.9 g Total Fat (1.6 g Mono, 0.8 g Poly, 0.3 g Sat); 15 mg Cholesterol;
16 g Carbohydrate; trace Fibre; 2 g Protein; 150 mg Sodium*

Pictured on page 90.

(continued on next page)

Note: Line 1/4 cup (60 mL) measure with plastic wrap to prevent rice mixture from sticking.

Variation: For spicier patties, add 1 tbsp. (15 mL) chopped fresh jalapeño pepper.

Spiced Brown Rice Bake

Rice has been restricted to a humble base for stir-fries and curries for too long! Celebrate this popular grain by seasoning it with the warm spices of ginger, cinnamon and cumin and tossing it with tender butternut squash.

Diced butternut (or buttercup) squash	2 cups	500 mL
Long grain brown rice	1 cup	250 mL
Cooking oil	2 tsp.	10 mL
Chopped onion	1 cup	250 mL
Garlic cloves, minced	2	2
(or 1/2 tsp., 2 mL, powder)		
Ground cinnamon	1/4 tsp.	1 mL
Ground cumin	1/4 tsp.	1 mL
Ground ginger	1/4 tsp.	1 mL
Salt	1/2 tsp.	2 mL
Pepper	1/4 tsp.	1 mL
Prepared vegetable broth	2 1/2 cups	625 mL

Combine squash and rice in greased 2 quart (2 L) casserole. Set aside.

Heat cooking oil in medium saucepan on medium. Add next 7 ingredients. Cook for 5 to 10 minutes, stirring often, until onion is softened.

Add broth. Bring to a boil. Add to rice mixture. Stir. Bake, covered, in 375°F (190°C) oven for about 75 minutes until rice is tender and liquid is absorbed. Fluff with fork. Let stand, covered, for 5 minutes. Makes about 4 1/2 cups (1.1 L).

1 cup (250 mL): 245 Calories; 3.4 g Total Fat (1.7 g Mono, 1.1 g Poly, 0.4 g Sat); 0 mg Cholesterol; 50 g Carbohydrate; 5 g Fibre; 5 g Protein; 795 mg Sodium

Moroccan Barley

Everyone will enjoy the sweet flavours of this homey dish.
Serve with beef or curried pork, chicken or lamb.

Finely chopped onion	1 cup	250 mL
Pot barley	1 1/2 cups	375 mL
Chopped dried apricot	2/3 cup	150 mL
Dark raisins	2/3 cup	150 mL
Ground cumin	1/2 tsp.	2 mL
Ground ginger	1/2 tsp.	2 mL
Garlic powder	1/4 tsp.	1 mL
Ground cinnamon	1/4 tsp.	1 mL
Salt	1/2 tsp.	2 mL
Pepper	1/4 tsp.	1 mL
Prepared vegetable broth	4 1/2 cups	1.1 L

Layer first 4 ingredients, in order given, in 3 quart (3 L) slow cooker.

Combine next 6 ingredients in small cup. Sprinkle over raisins.

Add broth. Do not stir. Cook, covered, on Low for 5 to 6 hours or on High 2 1/2 to 3 hours. Makes about 6 cups (1.5 L).

1 cup (250 mL): 282 Calories; 1.2 g Total Fat (trace Mono, 0.1 g Poly, trace Sat); 0 mg Cholesterol; 62 g Carbohydrate; 10 g Fibre; 7 g Protein; 1066 mg Sodium

Coconut Rice

Why make plain rice to serve with grilled chicken, pork or shrimp when you can just as easily make this flavourful coconut sensation?

Can of light coconut milk	14 oz.	398 mL
Water	1/4 cup	60 mL
White basmati rice	1 cup	250 mL
Cinnamon stick (4 inches, 10 cm)	1	1
Salt	1/2 tsp.	2 mL
Medium unsweetened coconut, toasted (see Tip, page 128), optional	1 tbsp.	15 mL

(continued on next page)

Combine coconut milk and water in medium saucepan. Bring to a boil. Add next 3 ingredients. Stir. Reduce heat to medium-low. Simmer, covered, for 15 minutes, without stirring. Remove from heat. Let stand, covered, for about 5 minutes until rice is tender and liquid is absorbed. Remove and discard cinnamon stick. Fluff with fork.

Sprinkle with coconut. Makes about 3 cups (750 mL).

1 cup (250 mL): 328 Calories; 9.3 g Total Fat (0.2 g Mono, 0.3 g Poly, 7.5 g Sat); 0 mg Cholesterol; 57 g Carbohydrate; trace Fibre; 5 g Protein; 393 mg Sodium

Hearty Rice Salad

Some things are better with time, and this salad is one of them! Enjoy its cool, fresh flavours right away or save it for the next day to let the flavours mingle.

Prepared chicken broth	1 cup	250 mL
Water	1 cup	250 mL
Long grain white rice	1 cup	250 mL
Can of mixed beans, rinsed and drained	19 oz.	540 mL
Diced tomato	1 cup	250 mL
Green onions, sliced	2	2
Real bacon bits (or 2 bacon slices, cooked crisp and crumbled)	2 tbsp.	30 mL
Italian dressing	1/4 cup	60 mL
Garlic clove, minced	1	1
Pepper	1/2 tsp.	2 mL

Combine broth and water in large saucepan. Bring to a boil. Add rice. Stir. Reduce heat to medium-low. Simmer, covered, for 15 minutes, without stirring. Remove from heat. Let stand, covered, for about 5 minutes until rice is tender and liquid is absorbed. Fluff with fork. Spread evenly on ungreased baking sheet with sides. Cool for 10 minutes. Transfer to large bowl.

Add next 4 ingredients. Toss gently.

Combine remaining 3 ingredients in small cup. Drizzle over rice mixture. Toss. Chill, covered, for 1 to 2 hours until cold. Makes about 6 cups (1.5 L).

1 cup (250 mL): 328 Calories; 8.6 g Total Fat (4.3 g Mono, 2.8 g Poly, 0.9 g Sat); 8 mg Cholesterol; 51 g Carbohydrate; 7 g Fibre; 12 g Protein; 526 mg Sodium

Pictured on page 144.

Baked Curry Risotto

A risotto for the 21st century! There's no need to stand around stirring because this Asian-flavoured risotto cooks gently in your oven while you take care of other things. Serve with a stir-fry of beef, pork or chicken.

Can of light coconut milk	14 oz.	398 mL
Prepared vegetable broth	1 cup	250 mL
Cooking oil	1 tsp.	5 mL
Chopped onion	1 cup	250 mL
Garlic cloves, minced	2	2
(or 1/2 tsp., 2 mL, powder)		
Finely grated gingerroot	1/2 tsp.	2 mL
Red curry paste	1/2 tsp.	2 mL
Salt	1/2 tsp.	2 mL
Pepper	1/4 tsp.	1 mL
Arborio rice	1 cup	250 mL
Finely chopped red pepper	1 cup	250 mL
Frozen peas	1 cup	250 mL
Grated lime zest	2 tsp.	10 mL

Combine coconut milk and broth in small saucepan. Cook on medium for about 5 minutes, stirring occasionally, until hot, but not boiling. Reduce heat to low. Cover to keep hot.

Heat cooking oil in large frying pan on medium. Add next 6 ingredients. Cook for 5 to 10 minutes, stirring occasionally, until onion is softened.

Add rice and red pepper. Stir. Transfer to greased 2 quart (2 L) casserole. Add broth mixture. Stir. Bake, covered, in 400°F (205°C) oven for about 35 minutes until rice is tender.

Add peas. Stir for 2 to 3 minutes until mixture starts to thicken. Let stand, covered, for about 5 minutes until liquid is absorbed.

Add lime zest. Stir. Makes about 4 cups (1 L).

1 cup (250 mL): 214 Calories; 7.9 g Total Fat (0.7 g Mono, 0.5 g Poly, 5.6 g Sat); 0 mg Cholesterol; 32 g Carbohydrate; 3 g Fibre; 4 g Protein; 602 mg Sodium

Greek Bulgur Pilaf

It's all Greek to us—and that's a good thing! We've seasoned tender bulgur with lots of fresh vegetables and the traditional flavours of lemon and oregano. Serve with chicken, pork or seafood.

Cooking oil	2 tsp.	10 mL
Chopped onion	1 cup	250 mL
Garlic cloves, minced	2	2
(or 1/2 tsp., 2 mL, powder)		
Diced red pepper	1 cup	250 mL
Diced zucchini (with peel)	1 cup	250 mL
Bulgur	3/4 cup	175 mL
Dried oregano	1/2 tsp.	2 mL
Salt	1/2 tsp.	2 mL
Pepper	1/4 tsp.	1 mL
Prepared vegetable broth	1 cup	250 mL
Grated lemon zest	2 tsp.	10 mL

Heat cooking oil in large saucepan on medium. Add onion and garlic. Cook for 5 to 10 minutes, stirring occasionally, until onion is softened.

Add red pepper and zucchini. Heat and stir for about 2 minutes until vegetables start to soften.

Add next 4 ingredients. Stir. Add broth. Bring to a boil. Reduce heat to medium. Cook, covered, for about 5 minutes until bulgur is tender and liquid is absorbed.

Add lemon zest. Stir. Makes about 3 cups (750 mL).

1 cup (250 mL): 198 Calories; 3.8 g Total Fat (1.9 g Mono, 1.2 g Poly, 0.4 g Sat); 0 mg Cholesterol; 38 g Carbohydrate; 6 g Fibre; 6 g Protein; 716 mg Sodium

Traditional Fried Rice

Fried rice is one of those homey, comforting dishes liked by just about everybody.
Prepare the rice ahead of time so it's cold—it fries much better that way!

Cooking oil	2 tsp.	10 mL
Large eggs, fork-beaten	2	2
Cooking oil	1 tbsp.	15 mL
Thinly sliced fresh white mushrooms	1 cup	250 mL
Finely chopped celery	1/2 cup	125 mL
Finely chopped onion	1/2 cup	125 mL
Cold cooked long grain white rice (about 1 cup, 250 mL, uncooked), see Tip, page 85	3 cups	750 mL
Frozen peas, thawed	1/2 cup	125 mL
Chopped green onion	1/4 cup	60 mL
Soy sauce	2 tbsp.	30 mL

Heat first amount of cooking oil in large frying pan or wok on medium-high. Add egg. Cook for about 30 seconds, without stirring, until almost set. Turn. Cook for about 30 seconds until set. Transfer to cutting board. Roll-up, jelly-roll style. Cut into thin slices. Set aside.

Heat second amount of cooking oil in same frying pan on medium. Add next 3 ingredients. Stir-fry for 2 to 4 minutes until onion is softened and liquid is evaporated.

Add rice. Stir-fry for about 1 minute until heated through.

Add remaining 3 ingredients and egg. Stir-fry for about 1 minute until heated through. Makes about 4 cups (1 L).

1 cup (250 mL): 271 Calories; 8.7 g Total Fat (4.5 g Mono, 2.2 g Poly, 1.3 g Sat); 93 mg Cholesterol; 39 g Carbohydrate; 2 g Fibre; 8 g Protein; 220 mg Sodium

Rice & Grains

Roasted Fennel Ratatouille

This fabulous blend of roasted veggies and tomatoes is great as a side for roasted chicken, or spoon it over couscous as part of a meatless meal.

Olive (or cooking) oil	2 tbsp.	30 mL
Garlic clove, minced	1	1
(or 1/4 tsp., 1 mL, powder)		
Dried basil	1 tsp.	5 mL
Dried thyme	1 tsp.	5 mL
Dried crushed chilies	1/4 tsp.	1 mL
Pepper	1/4 tsp.	1 mL
Medium fennel bulbs (white part only), cut into 8 wedges each	2	2
Medium onion, cut into 8 wedges	1	1
Can of diced tomatoes (with juice)	14 oz.	398 mL
Prepared vegetable broth	1/2 cup	125 mL
Dry (or alcohol-free) red wine	1/4 cup	60 mL
Tomato paste (see Tip, below)	1 tbsp.	15 mL

Chopped fresh basil, for garnish

Combine first 6 ingredients in large bowl.

Add fennel and onion. Toss until coated. Transfer to ungreased baking sheet with sides. Bake in 450°F (230°C) oven for about 20 minutes until softened and browned. Transfer to large frying pan.

Add next 4 ingredients. Stir. Bring to a boil on medium. Boil gently, covered, for 10 minutes, stirring occasionally, to blend flavours.

Garnish with basil. Makes about 4 cups (1 L).

1 cup (250 mL): 148 Calories; 7.2 g Total Fat (5.0 g Mono, 0.6 g Poly, 0.9 g Sat); 0 mg Cholesterol; 18 g Carbohydrate; 5 g Fibre; 3 g Protein; 396 mg Sodium

Pictured on page 144.

 tip If a recipe calls for less than an entire can of tomato paste, freeze the unopened can for 30 minutes. Open both ends and push the contents through one end. Slice off only what you need. Freeze the remaining paste in a resealable freezer bag or plastic wrap for future use.

Cilantro Lime Mushrooms

*Tender, smoky grilled mushrooms gain a refreshing tartness from
cilantro and lime juice. Serve with grilled steak or chicken.*

Fresh cilantro, lightly packed	1 cup	250 mL
Olive oil	1/4 cup	60 mL
Lime juice	1 tbsp.	15 mL
Garlic clove (or 1/4 tsp., 1 mL, powder)	1	1
Salt	1/2 tsp.	2 mL
Pepper	1/4 tsp.	1 mL
Fresh small whole white mushrooms	36	36
Bamboo skewers (8 inches, 20 cm, each), soaked in water for 10 minutes	4	4

Process first 6 ingredients with hand blender or in blender until smooth.
Divide into 2 small bowls. Set 1 bowl aside.

Preheat gas barbecue to medium-high. Thread mushrooms onto skewers.
Brush with cilantro mixture. Place on greased grill. Cook for 5 to 8 minutes,
turning once, until mushrooms are softened and browned. Transfer
mushrooms from skewers to medium bowl. Drizzle with reserved cilantro
mixture. Toss until coated. Serves 4.

*1 serving: 150 Calories; 13.7 g Total Fat (9.9 g Mono, 1.1 g Poly, 1.8 g Sat); 0 mg Cholesterol;
5 g Carbohydrate; trace Fibre; 2 g Protein; 303 mg Sodium*

Chili Garlic Cauliflower

*Tender cauliflower dressed in a creamy chili and garlic sauce
is a dynamite accompaniment for salmon or halibut.*

Roasted garlic mayonnaise	1/2 cup	125 mL
Finely chopped fresh cilantro	1 tbsp.	15 mL
Chili paste (sambal oelek)	1/4 tsp.	1 mL
Cauliflower florets	2 cups	500 mL
Water	2 tbsp.	30 mL

Combine first 3 ingredients in small bowl.

(continued on next page)

Vegetables

Put cauliflower and water into large microwave-safe bowl. Microwave, covered, on high (100%) for 4 to 6 minutes until tender. Drain well. Drizzle with mayonnaise mixture. Toss. Makes about 2 cups (500 mL).

1 cup (250 mL): 425 Calories; 44.1 g Total Fat (12.0 g Mono, 24.1 g Poly, 8.0 g Sat); 76 mg Cholesterol; 5 g Carbohydrate; 3 g Fibre; 2 g Protein; 161 mg Sodium

Variation: Try bacon and tomato-flavoured, lemon-flavoured or regular mayonnaise instead of roasted garlic mayonnaise.

Chilled Basil Orange Beans

Tender-crisp green beans are dressed with the fresh, vibrant flavours of orange and basil. Their fresh sweetness pairs perfectly with grilled meats.

Fresh (or frozen) whole green beans, halved crosswise (about 7 cups, 1.75 L)	1 1/2 lbs.	680 g
Chopped fresh basil	1/4 cup	60 mL
Finely chopped red onion	1/4 cup	60 mL
Olive oil	1/4 cup	60 mL
Orange juice	1/4 cup	60 mL
Garlic clove, minced (or 1/4 tsp., 1 mL, powder)	1	1
Dijon mustard	1 tsp.	5 mL
Grated orange zest	1 tsp.	5 mL
Salt	1/4 tsp.	1 mL
Pepper	1/4 tsp.	1 mL

Blanch green beans in boiling water in large saucepan for about 5 minutes (see Note) until bright green and tender-crisp. Drain. Immediately plunge into ice water in large bowl. Let stand for 10 minutes. Drain well. Transfer to large bowl.

Combine remaining 9 ingredients in jar with tight-fitting lid. Shake well. Drizzle over beans. Toss. Chill, covered, for 1 hour. Makes about 6 cups (1.5 L).

1 cup (250 mL): 129 Calories; 9.0 g Total Fat (6.6 g Mono, 0.8 g Poly, 1.2 g Sat); 0 mg Cholesterol; 10 g Carbohydrate; 3 g Fibre; 3 g Protein; 109 mg Sodium

Note: If using frozen green beans, blanch for 1 minute.

Grilled Asparagus

Sesame oil and chili paste jazz up this simple side for grilled meats.
Soaking the asparagus helps to keep it from scorching on the grill.

Fresh asparagus, trimmed of tough ends	1 lb.	454 g
Sesame oil (for flavour)	1 tbsp.	15 mL
Chili paste (sambal oelek)	1/4 tsp.	1 mL

Salt, sprinkle

Soak asparagus in cold water in large bowl for 30 minutes. Drain. Pat dry with paper towels. Place asparagus on large plate.

Combine sesame oil and chili paste in small cup. Brush asparagus with oil mixture. Preheat gas barbecue to medium. Place asparagus crosswise on greased grill. Cook for about 5 minutes, turning occasionally, until tender-crisp.

Sprinkle with salt. Serves 6.

1 serving: 209 Calories; 13.9 g Total Fat (5.3 g Mono, 5.9 g Poly, 2.1 g Sat); 0 mg Cholesterol; 18 g Carbohydrate; 9 g Fibre; 10 g Protein; 31 mg Sodium

Pictured on page 107.

Grilled Peppery Plantain

This ideal side for jerk pork or chicken is mildly sweet with a big peppery bite.

Semi-ripe plantains (see Note)	2	2
Sesame oil (for flavour)	1 tbsp.	15 mL
Cayenne pepper	1/4 tsp.	1 mL

Cut and discard ends of plantains. Slit peel lengthwise along inside curve, being careful not to cut into flesh. Remove and discard peel. Cut plantains in half crosswise. Cut pieces in half lengthwise.

Combine sesame oil and cayenne pepper in medium bowl. Add plantain Toss until coated. Preheat gas barbecue to medium-high. Cook plantain on greased grill for 2 to 4 minutes per side until tender. Makes 8 pieces.

(continued on next page)

1 piece: 70 Calories; 1.8 g Total Fat (0.7 g Mono, 0.7 g Poly, 0.3 g Sat); 0 mg Cholesterol; 14 g Carbohydrate; 1 g Fibre; 1 g Protein; 2 mg Sodium

Pictured on page 107.

Note: Green plantains are unripe; light yellow plantains with few or no black spots are semi-ripe; black plantains are ripe. Grocery stores usually carry unripened plantains. To ripen, store in brown paper bag at room temperature. It usually takes 7 to 8 days to fully ripen.

Cajun Breaded Eggplant

The crisp, well-seasoned coating on these tender eggplant slices provides a touch of fiery heat for those who like to spice things up every once in awhile. Serve with chicken or fish.

Large eggs	2	2
Louisiana hot sauce	2 tsp.	10 mL
Cajun seasoning	1 tsp.	5 mL
Medium peeled eggplant, cut crosswise into 1/4 inch (6 mm) slices	1	1
All-purpose flour	1/4 cup	60 mL
Fine dry bread crumbs	1/4 cup	60 mL
Yellow cornmeal	1/4 cup	60 mL
Cajun seasoning	1 tsp.	5 mL
Salt	1/2 tsp.	2 mL
Cooking oil	2 tbsp.	30 mL

Whisk first 3 ingredients in large bowl until frothy.

Add eggplant slices. Stir until coated. Let stand for 10 minutes.

Combine next 5 ingredients in medium bowl. Press both sides of eggplant slices into crumb mixture until coated.

Heat 1 tbsp. (15 mL) cooking oil in large frying pan on medium. Add half of eggplant slices. Cook for 2 to 4 minutes until golden. Turn slices over. Cook for about 2 minutes until golden. Remove to large plate. Cover to keep warm. Repeat with remaining cooking oil and eggplant slices. Serve immediately. Serves 4.

1 serving: 189 Calories; 9.9 g Total Fat (5.3 g Mono, 2.6 g Poly, 1.4 g Sat); 93 mg Cholesterol; 20 g Carbohydrate; 3 g Fibre; 6 g Protein; 596 mg Sodium

Soy Edamame

Edamame (pronounced ed-ah-MAH-may) is a side with pure Japanese chic. Made from young soybeans in their pods, they're eaten in the same manner as artichoke: serve them in their pods and your guests will run their teeth down the length of the pod, squeezing the pea-like edamame into their mouths. Serve with soup, salad, or grilled pork, chicken or fish.

Water	6 cups	1.5 L
Salt	1/2 tsp.	2 mL
Frozen unshelled edamame (soybeans)	1 lb.	454 g
Soy sauce	2 tbsp.	30 mL
Rice vinegar	1 tbsp.	15 mL
Sesame oil (for flavour)	1 tbsp.	15 mL
Pepper	1/4 tsp.	1 mL

Combine water and salt in large saucepan or Dutch oven. Bring to a boil. Add edamame. Reduce heat to medium. Boil gently, uncovered, for 5 minutes. Drain. Return to same pot.

Add remaining 4 ingredients. Toss. Transfer to serving bowl. Makes about 3 1/2 cups (875 mL).

1 cup (250 mL): 212 Calories; 8.1 g Total Fat (1.5 g Mono, 1.6 g Poly, 0.5 g Sat); 0 mg Cholesterol; 16 g Carbohydrate; 2 g Fibre; 18 g Protein; 572 mg Sodium

Pictured at right.

1. Grilled Peppery Plantain, page 104
2. Grilled Asparagus, page 104
3. Soy Edamame, above

Props courtesy of: Stokes

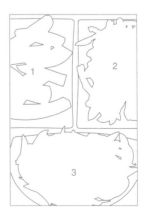

Vegetables

Daikon Salad

If you like red radishes, you'll love daikon! This salad complements daikon's crisp, peppery bite with an "Asian-fusion" dressing.

Thinly sliced daikon radish, cut in half	2 cups	500 mL
Thinly sliced carrot	1 cup	250 mL
Thinly sliced English cucumber (with peel)	1 cup	250 mL
Thinly sliced red pepper	1/2 cup	125 mL
Coarsely chopped fresh mint	1/4 cup	60 mL
Sliced green onion	2 tbsp.	30 mL
Lime juice	2 tbsp.	30 mL
Rice vinegar	2 tbsp.	30 mL
Sweet chili sauce	2 tbsp.	30 mL
Sesame oil	2 tsp.	10 mL
Finely grated gingerroot	1 tsp.	5 mL
Granulated sugar	1 tsp.	5 mL

Combine first 6 ingredients in large bowl.

Whisk remaining 6 ingredients in small bowl. Drizzle over daikon mixture. Toss. Makes about 4 cups (1 L).

1 cup (250 mL): 75 Calories; 3.4 g Total Fat (0.9 g Mono, 1.0 g Poly, 0.4 g Sat); 0 mg Cholesterol; 11 g Carbohydrate; 2 g Fibre; 2 g Protein; 264 mg Sodium

Pictured at left.

1. Brussels Sprouts With Bacon, page 110
2. Daikon Salad, above

Props courtesy of: Casa Bugatti
Stokes

Brussels Sprouts With Bacon

Everything's better with bacon! These smoky-flavoured,
tender Brussels sprouts are great with steak.

Water	1/2 cup	125 mL
Garlic cloves, minced	2	2
(or 1/2 tsp., 2 mL, powder)		
Lemon pepper	1/2 tsp.	2 mL
Fresh (or frozen) Brussels sprouts	4 cups	1 L
(see Note)		
Bacon slices, cooked crisp and crumbled	5	5
Butter (or hard margarine)	1 tbsp.	15 mL

Combine first 3 ingredients in large saucepan. Bring to a boil. Add Brussels sprouts. Cook, covered, on medium for 8 to 10 minutes until tender.

Add bacon and butter. Stir until butter is melted. Makes about 3 cups (750 mL).

1 cup (250 mL): 144 Calories; 8.6 g Total Fat (3.0 g Mono, 0.8 g Poly, 3.9 g Sat); 22 mg Cholesterol; 11 g Carbohydrate; 5 g Fibre; 8 g Protein; 354 mg Sodium

Pictured on page 108.

Note: If using fresh Brussels sprouts, remove and discard any wilted outer leaves. Cut an "x" in bottom of stems. If using frozen sprouts, reduce cooking time by half.

Paré Pointer

Do bakers cover their beds with cookie sheets?

Rutabaga Cornmeal Puff

*The humble rutabaga (or yellow turnip) is transformed into a light
and delicate, yet homey dish that provides a lovely complement
to a heavier main course of ham or corned beef.*

Chopped peeled yellow turnip (rutabaga)	5 cups	1.25 L
Salt	1/2 tsp.	2 mL
Egg whites (large), room temperature	2	2
Egg yolks (large), fork-beaten	2	2
Yellow cornmeal	1/4 cup	60 mL
Butter (or hard margarine), melted	2 tbsp.	30 mL
Brown sugar, packed	1 tbsp.	15 mL
Salt	1/2 tsp.	2 mL
Pepper	1/4 tsp.	1 mL
Dried rosemary, crushed	1/8 tsp.	0.5 mL

Pour water into large saucepan until about 1 inch (2.5 cm) deep.
Add turnip and salt. Cover. Bring to a boil. Reduce heat to medium.
Cook for 12 to 15 minutes until tender. Drain well. Mash.

Beat egg whites in medium bowl until stiff peaks form.

Combine remaining 7 ingredients in large bowl. Add turnip. Beat until
smooth. Fold in egg whites until no white streaks remain. Spread evenly
in greased 1 1/2 quart (1.5 L) casserole. Bake in 350°F (175°C) oven for
about 40 minutes until puffed and golden. Serve immediately. Makes
about 5 cups (1.25 L).

*1 cup (250 mL): 172 Calories; 7.1 g Total Fat (2.1 g Mono, 0.7 g Poly, 3.6 g Sat); 88 mg Cholesterol;
23 g Carbohydrate; trace Fibre; 5 g Protein; 326 mg Sodium*

Spinach-Stuffed Acorn Squash

Experience the best of the fall harvest with this savoury take on acorn squash.
This dish is a natural partner for roast turkey or chicken.

Small acorn squash (about 1 lb., 454 g, each)	3	3
Water	1/4 cup	60 mL
Butter (or hard margarine)	1 tbsp.	15 mL
Chopped fresh white mushrooms	1 1/2 cups	375 mL
Diced carrot	1/4 cup	60 mL
Diced onion	1/4 cup	60 mL
Prepared chicken broth	1/2 cup	125 mL
Box of frozen chopped spinach, thawed and squeezed dry	10 oz.	300 g
Cooked rice (about 1/3 cup, 75 mL, uncooked)	1 cup	250 mL
Chopped dark raisins	1/4 cup	60 mL
Chopped walnuts, toasted (see Tip, page 128)	1/4 cup	60 mL
Dried oregano	1/2 tsp.	2 mL
Salt	1/2 tsp.	2 mL
Pepper	1/4 tsp.	1 mL
Feta cheese, crumbled	1/2 cup	125 mL

Cut squash in half lengthwise. Remove seeds. Place 3 halves, cut-side down, in ungreased 3 quart (3 L) casserole. Add half of water. Microwave, covered, on high (100%) for about 10 minutes until almost tender. Drain. Repeat with remaining squash and water. Arrange cooked squash, cut-side up, on baking sheet.

Melt butter in large frying pan on medium-high. Add next 3 ingredients. Cook for 5 to 10 minutes, stirring occasionally, until vegetables are softened.

Add broth. Stir. Add next 7 ingredients. Heat and stir for 2 to 4 minutes until heated through.

Add cheese. Stir. Spoon into squash halves. Bake, uncovered, in 400°F (205°C) oven for about 20 minutes until squash is tender and cheese is melted. Makes 6 stuffed squash.

1 stuffed squash: 170 Calories; 8.4 g Total Fat (1.6 g Mono, 2.7 g Poly, 3.5 g Sat); 17 mg Cholesterol; 20 g Carbohydrate; 3 g Fibre; 6 g Protein; 519 mg Sodium

Bean Sprout Slaw

*We've given this unique coleslaw an Asian twist with
bean sprouts and a hoisin-flavoured mayonnaise dressing.*

Water	12 cups	3 L
Fresh bean sprouts	3 cups	750 mL
Mayonnaise	1/4 cup	60 mL
Hoisin sauce	2 tbsp.	30 mL
Rice vinegar	1 tbsp.	15 mL
Dried crushed chilies	1/4 tsp.	1 mL
Pepper	1/4 tsp.	1 mL
Coleslaw mix	1 cup	250 mL
Julienned peeled jicama (see Tip, below)	1 cup	250 mL
Grated carrot	1/2 cup	125 mL

Measure water into Dutch oven or large pot. Bring to a boil. Add bean
sprouts. Cook, uncovered, for 30 seconds. Drain. Rinse with cold water
until cooled completely. Drain well.

Whisk next 5 ingredients in medium bowl.

Add remaining 3 ingredients and bean sprouts. Toss until coated.
Makes about 4 cups (1 L).

*1 cup (250 mL): 203 Calories; 11.7 g Total Fat (0.2 g Mono, 0.3 g Poly, 1.6 g Sat); 5 mg Cholesterol;
22 g Carbohydrate; 5 g Fibre; 6 g Protein; 242 mg Sodium*

 tip   To julienne, cut into very thin strips that resemble matchsticks.

Kohlrabi Apple Slaw

The crisp texture of kohlrabi is perfectly suited for coleslaw—and mixed with a mustard cream dressing, it's a great complement to grilled burgers, hot dogs or chicken.

Half-and-half cream	1/4 cup	60 mL
Chopped fresh parsley	2 tbsp.	30 mL
(or 1 1/2 tsp., 7 mL, flakes)		
Lemon juice	2 tbsp.	30 mL
Dijon mustard (with whole seeds)	1 tbsp.	15 mL
Granulated sugar	1/2 tsp.	2 mL
Salt	1/4 tsp.	1 mL
Pepper	1/4 tsp.	1 mL
Grated peeled kohlrabi	4 cups	1 L
Grated unpeeled tart apple	1 cup	250 mL
(such as Granny Smith)		

Whisk first 7 ingredients in small bowl.

Add kohlrabi and apple. Stir. Makes about 4 cups (1 L).

1 cup (250 mL): 84 Calories; 2.3 g Total Fat (0.6 g Mono, 0.2 g Poly, 1.2 g Sat); 6 mg Cholesterol; 16 g Carbohydrate; 1 g Fibre; 3 g Protein; 259 mg Sodium

Ginger-Glazed Parsnips

Would your family gladly forgo their veggies for a sugary treat? Appeal to their sweeter side with these orange and ginger-glazed parsnips. Serve with roast beef, pork or chicken.

Orange juice	2/3 cup	150 mL
Water	1/4 cup	60 mL
Apple cider vinegar	2 tbsp.	30 mL
Ground ginger	1 tsp.	5 mL
Sliced parsnip (1/4 inch, 6 mm, thick)	3 cups	750 mL
Orange juice	2 tbsp.	30 mL
Brown sugar, packed	1 tbsp.	15 mL

(continued on next page)

Combine first 4 ingredients in medium frying pan. Bring to a boil on medium. Add parsnip. Cook, partially covered, for 15 to 20 minutes, stirring occasionally, until parsnip is tender.

Add second amount of orange juice and brown sugar. Stir. Reduce heat to medium-low. Cook, uncovered, for about 2 minutes, stirring occasionally, until parsnip is glazed. Makes about 2 1/2 cups (625 mL).

1 cup (250 mL): 180 Calories; 0.7 g Total Fat (0.2 g Mono, 0.1 g Poly, 0.1 g Sat); 0 mg Cholesterol; 43 g Carbohydrate; 5 g Fibre; 3 g Protein; 20 mg Sodium

Presto Pesto Zucchini

Need a veggie side that's ready lickety-split? This Mediterranean-inspired dish packed with zucchini and tomato fits the bill! For colour contrast, use a mix of green and yellow zucchini.

Finely chopped onion	2 tbsp.	30 mL
Butter (or hard margarine)	1 tbsp.	15 mL
Cubed zucchini (with peel)	4 cups	1 L
Tomato sauce	1/4 cup	60 mL
Basil pesto	2 tbsp.	30 mL
Chopped Roma (plum) tomatoes	2 cups	500 mL
Grated Asiago cheese	1/4 cup	60 mL
Salt	1/4 tsp.	1 mL
Pepper	1/4 tsp.	1 mL

Put onion and butter into ungreased 2 quart (2 L) casserole. Microwave, covered, on high (100%) for about 2 minutes until onion is softened.

Add next 3 ingredients. Toss. Microwave, covered, on high (100%) for about 8 minutes until zucchini is tender-crisp.

Add tomato. Stir. Microwave, covered, on high (100%) for 2 to 4 minutes until heated through.

Add remaining 3 ingredients. Stir. Microwave, covered, for 30 seconds. Let stand for 2 minutes. Makes about 5 cups (1.25 L).

1 cup (250 mL): 101 Calories; 6.5 g Total Fat (1.2 g Mono, 1.1 g Poly, 2.8 g Sat); 11 mg Cholesterol; 9 g Carbohydrate; 3 g Fibre; 4 g Protein; 343 mg Sodium

Orange Ginger Kale

All hail kale! It's colourful, it's tasty, and it keeps its texture even after cooking.
This king among greens needs only a simple dressing of orange, ginger and soy.

Cooking oil	1 tsp.	5 mL
Garlic cloves, minced	2	2
(or 1/2 tsp., 2 mL, powder)		
Finely grated gingerroot	1 tsp.	5 mL
Orange juice	1/3 cup	75 mL
Rice vinegar	1 tbsp.	15 mL
Soy sauce	2 tsp.	10 mL
Brown sugar, packed	1 tsp.	5 mL
Pepper	1/4 tsp.	1 mL
Chopped kale leaves, lightly packed	10 cups	2.5 L
(see Tip, page 64)		

Heat cooking oil in Dutch oven on medium. Add garlic and ginger. Heat and stir for about 1 minute until fragrant. Add next 5 ingredients. Stir. Bring to a boil.

Add kale. Stir until starting to wilt. Cook, covered, for about 10 minutes until tender. Makes about 4 cups (1 L).

1 cup (250 mL): 112 Calories; 2.4 g Total Fat (0.8 g Mono, 0.9 g Poly, 0.2 g Sat); 0 mg Cholesterol; 21 g Carbohydrate; 4 g Fibre; 6 g Protein; 205 mg Sodium

Paré Pointer

The race was on! The cabbage was ahead, the tap
was running and the tomato tried to ketchup.

Roasted Beets

Forget boiling them, roasting brings out the natural sweetness of fresh beets.
Serve with barbecued chicken or grilled pork chops.

Fresh medium unpeeled beets, scrubbed clean and trimmed	1 1/2 lbs.	680 g
Olive oil	3 tbsp.	50 mL
Balsamic vinegar	2 tbsp.	30 mL
Brown sugar, packed	1 tsp.	5 mL
Dried tarragon	1 tsp.	5 mL
Salt	1/4 tsp.	1 mL
Pepper	1/8 tsp.	0.5 mL

Preheat gas barbecue to high. Wrap each beet in foil. Reduce heat to medium. Place beets on grill (see Note). Close lid. Cook for about 45 minutes, turning occasionally, until tender. Unwrap beets. Let stand until cool enough to handle. Peel beets (see Tip, below). Cut each beet into 8 wedges. Cover to keep warm.

Whisk remaining 6 ingredients in medium bowl. Add beets. Toss. Makes about 2 1/2 cups (625 mL).

1 cup (250 mL): 239 Calories; 16.5 g Total Fat (12.0 g Mono, 1.5 g Poly, 2.2 g Sat); 0 mg Cholesterol; 21 g Carbohydrate; 5 g Fibre; 3 g Protein; 381 mg Sodium

Note: Foil-wrapped beets can also be roasted in 400°F (205°C) oven until tender.

 tip Don't get caught red handed! Wear rubber gloves when handling beets.

Corn Custard

Custards need not be sweet. This one's full of the savoury flavours of cheese, chili and onion. This rich and creamy side goes great with beef, chicken or pork.

Large eggs, fork-beaten	4	4
Half-and-half cream	3/4 cup	175 mL
Finely chopped roasted red pepper, drained and blotted dry	1/4 cup	60 mL
Finely chopped green onion	2 tbsp.	30 mL
Chili powder	1/2 tsp.	2 mL
Salt	1/2 tsp.	2 mL
Pepper	1/4 tsp.	1 mL
Frozen kernel corn, thawed	2 cups	500 mL
Grated sharp Cheddar cheese	1/2 cup	125 mL

Combine first 7 ingredients in large bowl.

Add corn and cheese. Stir. Spread evenly in greased 8 x 8 inch (20 x 20 cm) pan. Place smaller pan in 9 x 13 inch (22 x 30 cm) pan. Carefully pour boiling water into larger pan until water comes halfway up side of smaller pan. Bake in 350°F (175°C) oven for 40 to 45 minutes until wooden pick inserted in centre comes out clean. Cuts into 6 pieces.

1 piece: 174 Calories; 10.5 g Total Fat (3.4 g Mono, 0.7 g Poly, 5.3 g Sat); 146 mg Cholesterol; 11 g Carbohydrate; 1 g Fibre; 9 g Protein; 347 mg Sodium

Herbed Lemon Peas

Looking for a lemony addition to a meal of pork, lamb, chicken or salmon? The math may be strange but we're sure you'll agree—four ingredients plus seven minutes equals one great side!

Frozen peas	3 cups	750 mL
Prepared vegetable broth	1/4 cup	60 mL
Italian seasoning	1 tsp.	5 mL
Grated lemon zest	1 tbsp.	15 mL

(continued on next page)

Combine peas and broth in small microwave-safe bowl. Microwave, covered, on high (100%) for 5 minutes.

Add Italian seasoning. Stir. Cook, uncovered, for about 2 minutes until peas are tender.

Add lemon zest. Stir. Makes about 2 1/2 cups (625 mL).

1 cup (250 mL): 138 Calories; 0.7 g Total Fat (0.1 g Mono, 0.3 g Poly, 0.1 g Sat); 0 mg Cholesterol; 25 g Carbohydrate; 8 g Fibre; 9 g Protein; 240 mg Sodium

Lemon Spinach And Leek

Truly the cream of the crop! Creamy spinach and leek are accented with lemon and Dijon to counterbalance the richness. A 1/2 cup (125 mL) serving is more than satisfying!

Olive (or cooking) oil	1 tsp.	5 mL
Thinly sliced leek (white part only)	1 cup	250 mL
Garlic clove, minced	1	1
(or 1/4 tsp., 1 mL, powder)		
Half-and-half cream	1/3 cup	75 mL
Dijon mustard	1 tsp.	5 mL
Salt	1/2 tsp.	2 mL
Pepper	1/4 tsp.	1 mL
Fresh spinach leaves, lightly packed	14 cups	3.5 L
Lemon juice	2 tsp.	10 mL

Heat olive oil in large frying pan on medium. Add leek and garlic. Cook for 5 to 10 minutes, stirring occasionally, until leek is tender.

Add next 4 ingredients. Heat and stir for 1 minute.

Add spinach and lemon juice. Cook for 2 to 3 minutes, tossing occasionally, until spinach is just wilted. Makes about 2 cups (500 mL).

1/2 cup (125 mL): 158 Calories; 8.1 g Total Fat (3.1 g Mono, 0.8 g Poly, 3.5 g Sat); 16 mg Cholesterol; 18 g Carbohydrate; 6 g Fibre; 8 g Protein; 812 mg Sodium

Cucumber Mango Salad

A decadently creamy salad dressed with lots of big crunchy walnut pieces and the flavours of maple and sour cream. Serve with beef, chicken, pork or seafood.

Sour cream	1/2 cup	125 mL
Maple (or maple-flavoured) syrup	2 tbsp.	30 mL
Ground ginger	1/2 tsp.	2 mL
Salt	1/4 tsp.	1 mL
Pepper	1/4 tsp.	1 mL
Thickly sliced English cucumber (with peel), quartered	2 cups	500 mL
Frozen mango pieces, thawed and drained, larger pieces halved	1 cup	250 mL
Walnut pieces, toasted (see Tip, page 128)	1 cup	250 mL

Combine first 5 ingredients in small bowl.

Add remaining 3 ingredients. Toss until coated. Makes about 4 cups (1 L).

1 cup (250 mL): 312 Calories; 25.0 g Total Fat (4.2 g Mono, 14.4 g Poly, 5.1 g Sat); 12 mg Cholesterol; 21 g Carbohydrate; 3 g Fibre; 6 g Protein; 164 mg Sodium

Bok Choy Stir-Fry

This quick and easy Asian-inspired, stir-fried side requires minimal prep and is ready in a flash.

Prepared chicken broth	1/4 cup	60 mL
Soy sauce	2 tsp.	10 mL
Cornstarch	1 tsp.	5 mL
Finely grated gingerroot	1 tsp.	5 mL
Pepper	1/4 tsp.	1 mL
Sesame (or cooking) oil	1 tsp.	5 mL
Chopped bok choy	8 cups	2 L
Garlic cloves, minced	2	2

Put first 5 ingredients into small cup. Stir until smooth. Set aside.

(continued on next page)

Heat wok or large frying pan on medium-high until very hot. Add sesame oil. Add bok choy and garlic. Stir-fry for 2 to 4 minutes until bok choy is tender-crisp. Stir soy sauce mixture. Add to bok choy mixture. Heat and stir for about 1 minute until boiling and slightly thickened. Makes about 3 cups (750 mL).

1 cup (250 mL): 48 Calories; 2.0 g Total Fat (0.7 g Mono, 0.8 g Poly, 0.3 g Sat); 0 mg Cholesterol; 6 g Carbohydrate; 2 g Fibre; 3 g Protein; 421 mg Sodium

Jicama Zucchini Salad

Jicama adds a unique crunch to this colourful salad. You can even make it the night before—the vegetables will retain their crispness even after a good soak in the dressing.

Julienned peeled jicama (see Tip, page 113)	3 cups	750 mL
Julienned carrot	1 1/2 cups	375 mL
Julienned small zucchini (with peel), see Note	1 1/2 cups	375 mL
Salted, roasted shelled pumpkin seeds	1/3 cup	75 mL
Chopped fresh parsley	2 tbsp.	30 mL
Poppy seeds	1 tbsp.	15 mL
Cooking oil	1/3 cup	75 mL
Balsamic vinegar	2 tbsp.	30 mL
Liquid honey	2 tbsp.	30 mL
Dijon mustard (with whole seeds)	1 tbsp.	15 mL
Salt	1/2 tsp.	2 mL
Pepper	1/4 tsp.	1 mL

Combine first 6 ingredients in large bowl.

Whisk remaining 6 ingredients in small bowl. Drizzle over vegetable mixture. Toss. Makes about 6 cups (1.5 L).

1 cup (250 mL): 205 Calories; 14.0 g Total Fat (7.4 g Mono, 4.0 g Poly, 1.1 g Sat); 0 mg Cholesterol; 19 g Carbohydrate; 5 g Fibre; 2 g Protein; 297 mg Sodium

Pictured on page 18.

Note: If using a larger zucchini, remove seeds before cutting into strips.

Baked Turnip

Potato wedges passé? Set your sights on a newer, more exciting root veggie!
These turnip wedges have more of a bite than their potato counterparts.
Serve with beef, chicken or pork.

Peeled purple-topped turnips	1 1/2 lbs.	680 g
Cooking oil	2 tbsp.	30 mL
Cajun seasoning	1 tsp.	5 mL
Salt	1/2 tsp.	2 mL
Pepper	1/2 tsp.	2 mL

Cut turnips into 1/2 inch (12 mm) thick wedges.

Combine remaining 4 ingredients in medium bowl. Add turnip. Toss until coated. Arrange in single layer on greased baking sheet with sides. Bake in 450°F (230°C) oven for about 15 minutes until tender and bottoms are browned. Serves 6.

1 serving: 72 Calories; 4.7 g Total Fat (2.7 g Mono, 1.4 g Poly, 0.3 g Sat); 0 mg Cholesterol;
7 g Carbohydrate; 2 g Fibre; 1 g Protein; 361 mg Sodium

Simple Swiss Chard

Expand your view of greens by forgoing the spinach tonight and
trying some garden-fresh chard. All you need are a few ingredients
and you'll have a delicious and versatile side that complements meat,
chicken or fish. This recipe works equally well with ruby chard.

Olive (or cooking) oil	2 tbsp.	30 mL
Garlic clove, minced	1	1
(or 1/4 tsp., 1 mL, powder)		
Chopped Swiss chard, lightly packed	8 cups	2 L
Ground nutmeg	1/4 tsp.	1 mL
Salt	1/4 tsp.	1 mL
Pepper	1/4 tsp.	1 mL
Grated Parmesan cheese	2 tbsp.	30 mL

(continued on next page)

Heat olive oil in large frying pan on medium-high. Add garlic. Heat and stir for 1 to 2 minutes until fragrant. Add Swiss chard. Heat and stir for 2 to 4 minutes until heated through and wilted.

Add next 3 ingredients. Stir. Transfer to serving dish.

Sprinkle with cheese. Makes about 2 cups (500 mL).

1 cup (250 mL): 181 Calories; 15.9 g Total Fat (10.0 g Mono, 1.2 g Poly, 2.9 g Sat); 5 mg Cholesterol; 6 g Carbohydrate; 2 g Fibre; 6 g Protein; 725 mg Sodium

Pictured on page 125.

Broccoli Pepper Salad

A fabulous side need not be complicated! This simple, yet elegant mix of crunchy vegetables with a bright lemon flavour will go well with most entrees. If you are making this salad in advance, hold off on adding the lemon juice until just before serving.

Broccoli florets	5 cups	1.25 L
Coarsely grated carrot	2/3 cup	150 mL
Thinly sliced red pepper	2/3 cup	150 mL
Thinly sliced yellow pepper	2/3 cup	150 mL
Thinly sliced red onion	1/3 cup	75 mL
Olive oil	2 tbsp.	30 mL
Lemon juice	1 tbsp.	15 mL
Lemon pepper	1 1/2 tsp.	7 mL

Blanch broccoli in boiling salted water in large saucepan for 2 to 4 minutes until bright green. Drain. Immediately plunge into ice water in large bowl. Let stand for 5 minutes. Drain well. Transfer to separate large bowl.

Add next 4 ingredients. Toss.

Drizzle with olive oil and lemon juice. Sprinkle with lemon pepper. Toss. Makes about 8 cups (2 L).

1 cup (250 mL): 56 Calories; 3.6 g Total Fat (2.5 g Mono, 0.4 g Poly, 0.5 g Sat); 0 mg Cholesterol; 6 g Carbohydrate; 2 g Fibre; 2 g Protein; 79 mg Sodium

Pictured on page 125.

Curried Okra And Tomato

*Okra, a down-south fave, gets an Asian-inspired touch in the form of curry—
and the two worlds collide with amazing results. Serve with chicken or pork.*

Fresh (or frozen, thawed) okra	3 cups	750 mL
Cooking oil	2 tsp.	10 mL
Curry powder	1 tsp.	5 mL
Diced Roma (plum) tomato	1 cup	250 mL
Salt	1/2 tsp.	2 mL
Lime juice	1 tbsp.	15 mL

Rinse okra. Pat dry. Trim stem ends.

Heat cooking oil in large frying pan on medium. Add okra and curry
powder. Cook for about 5 minutes, stirring often, until browned.

Add tomato and salt. Heat and stir for about 2 minutes until tomato
is softened and okra is tender-crisp.

Add lime juice. Stir. Makes about 2 cups (500 mL).

*1 cup (250 mL): 113 Calories; 5.1 g Total Fat (2.8 g Mono, 1.6 g Poly, 0.4 g Sat); 0 mg Cholesterol;
16 g Carbohydrate; 6 g Fibre; 4 g Protein; 603 mg Sodium*

Pictured at right.

1. Broccoli Pepper Salad, page 123
2. Curried Okra And Tomato, above
3. Simple Swiss Chard, page 122

Props courtesy of: Mikasa Home Store

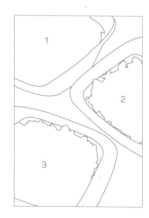

Vegetables

Sun-Dried Tomato Sugar Peas

Witness how opposites attract in this perfect pairing of bold
sun-dried tomatoes with mild, sweet sugar snap peas.
Serve with pork chops or grilled chicken breasts.

Sugar snap peas, trimmed	1 lb.	454 g
Garlic butter	2 tbsp.	30 mL
Sliced red onion	1/2 cup	125 mL
Sun-dried tomatoes in oil, blotted dry and chopped	1/4 cup	60 mL

Pour water into large saucepan until about 1 inch (2.5 cm) deep. Bring to a boil. Reduce heat to medium. Add sugar snap peas. Boil gently, covered, for about 5 minutes until bright green. Drain.

Melt garlic butter in large frying pan on medium. Add onion. Cook for about 5 minutes, stirring occasionally, until softened. Add snap peas and sun-dried tomato. Heat and stir for about 2 minutes until coated. Makes about 3 1/2 cups (875 mL).

1 cup (250 mL): 144 Calories; 7.4 g Total Fat (0.7 g Mono, 0.2 g Poly, 3.0 g Sat); 11 mg Cholesterol; 15 g Carbohydrate; 4 g Fibre; trace Protein; 100 mg Sodium

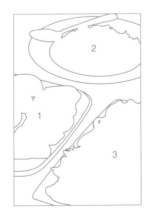

1. Tomato Pesto Biscotti, page 25
2. Tabbouleh, page 41
3. Sweet Peppers And Almonds, page 128

Props courtesy of: Casa Bugatti
Stokes

Vegetables

127

Sweet Peppers And Almonds

Sweet caramelized onion complements tender peppers and crunchy nuts.
Serve with grilled meats or baked ham. A 1/2 cup (125 mL)
serving of this tangy side goes a long way.

Cooking oil	1 tbsp.	15 mL
Thinly sliced onion	1 1/2 cups	375 mL
Balsamic vinegar	2 tbsp.	30 mL
Brown sugar, packed	2 tbsp.	30 mL
Sliced green pepper	1 cup	250 mL
Sliced red pepper	1 cup	250 mL
Sliced yellow pepper	1 cup	250 mL
Sliced natural almonds, toasted (see Tip, below)	1/2 cup	125 mL

Heat cooking oil in large frying pan on medium. Add onion. Cook for about 10 minutes, stirring occasionally, until caramelized.

Add vinegar and brown sugar. Heat and stir for 1 to 2 minutes until sugar is dissolved.

Add next 3 ingredients. Cook for about 5 minutes, stirring occasionally, until peppers are tender-crisp.

Add almonds. Stir. Makes about 2 1/2 cups (625 mL).

1/2 cup (125 mL): 146 Calories; 7.8 g Total Fat (4.7 g Mono, 2.1 g Poly, 0.6 g Sat); 0 mg Cholesterol; 18 g Carbohydrate; 3 g Fibre; 3 g Protein; 8 mg Sodium

Pictured on page 126 and back cover.

tip   When toasting nuts, seeds or coconut, cooking times will vary for each type of nut—so never toast them together. For small amounts, place ingredient in an ungreased frying pan. Heat on medium for 3 to 5 minutes, stirring often, until golden. For larger amounts, spread ingredient evenly in an ungreased shallow pan. Bake in a 350°F (175°C) oven for 5 to 10 minutes, stirring or shaking often, until golden.

Snow Pea Jicama Stir-Fry

Jicama makes an excellent substitute for water chestnuts in this colourful vegetable stir-fry. Serve with beef, chicken, pork or seafood.

Cooking oil	1 tsp.	5 mL
Thinly sliced onion	1/2 cup	125 mL
Garlic clove, minced	1	1
(or 1/4 tsp., 1 mL, powder)		
Italian seasoning	1 tsp.	5 mL
Bag of snow peas, trimmed	7 oz.	220 g
Thinly sliced red pepper	1 cup	250 mL
Peeled jicama, cut into	6 oz.	170 g
1/4 inch (6 mm) thick strips,		
2 inches (5 cm) long		
Water	1/4 cup	60 mL
Salt	1/2 tsp.	2 mL
Pepper	1/4 tsp.	1 mL
Grated lemon zest	1 tsp.	5 mL

Heat wok or large frying pan on medium-high until very hot. Add cooking oil. Add onion. Stir-fry for about 1 minute until softened. Add garlic and Italian seasoning. Stir-fry for about 30 seconds until fragrant.

Add next 3 ingredients. Stir-fry for 1 minute.

Add next 3 ingredients. Stir. Cook, covered, for about 2 minutes until snow peas are tender-crisp.

Add lemon zest. Toss. Makes about 4 cups (1 L).

1 cup (250 mL): 252 Calories; 5.6 g Total Fat (2.8 g Mono, 1.9 g Poly, 0.5 g Sat); 0 mg Cholesterol; 45 g Carbohydrate; 14 g Fibre; 9 g Protein; 1189 mg Sodium

Pictured on front cover.

Red Cabbage And Apricot Braise

If eye-popping colour is what you're looking for in a side,
you'll love the vivid purple-red and golden apricot in this
sweet and tangy dish. Serve with beef, pork or sausages.

Sliced onion	1 cup	250 mL
Red cabbage, cut into	2 lbs	900 g
1/2 inch (12 mm) thick slices		
Chopped dried apricot	1/2 cup	125 mL
Apple juice	1 cup	250 mL
Brown sugar, packed	1/4 cup	60 mL
Red wine vinegar	1/4 cup	60 mL
Salt	1/4 tsp.	1 mL
Pepper	1/4 tsp.	1 mL

Layer first 3 ingredients, in order given, in 4 quart (4 L) slow cooker.

Whisk remaining 5 ingredients in small bowl. Pour over apricot. Cook, covered, on Low for 7 to 8 hours or on High for 3 1/2 to 4 hours. Makes about 6 cups (1.5 L).

1 cup (250 mL): 114 Calories; 0.1 g Total Fat (trace Mono, 0.1 g Poly, trace Sat); 0 mg Cholesterol; 29 g Carbohydrate; 3 g Fibre; 2 g Protein; 128 mg Sodium

Sweet Jalapeño Tomatillos

Although tomatillos look like small green tomatoes wrapped in papery husks,
their tart taste is completely unique and lends itself well to a little jalapeño heat.
Serve with grilled chicken, pork or Mexican dishes.

Tomatillos	1 lb.	454 g
Green jalapeño jelly	1/3 cup	75 mL
Salt	1/4 tsp.	1 mL

Remove papery husks from tomatillos. Wash and pat dry. Preheat gas barbecue to medium-high. Cook tomatillos on ungreased grill for about 10 minutes, turning occasionally, until grill marks appear. Tomatillos should still be quite firm. Transfer to cutting board. Cut into quarters. Place in small serving bowl.

(continued on next page)

Combine jalapeño jelly and salt in small microwave-safe bowl. Microwave on medium (50%) for 20 to 30 seconds until melted. Stir. Drizzle over tomatillos. Makes about 2 cups (500 mL).

1 cup (250 mL): 182 Calories; 2.3 g Total Fat (0 g Mono, 1.0 g Poly, 0.3 g Sat); 0 mg Cholesterol; 46 g Carbohydrate; 0 g Fibre; 2 g Protein; 295 mg Sodium

Suey Choy Slaw

The mild flavour of suey choy in a light vinaigrette is a great alternative to those heavier, mayonnaise-based coleslaws.

Thinly sliced suey choy (Chinese cabbage)	4 cups	1 L
Julienned carrot (see Tip, page 113)	1 cup	250 mL
Thinly sliced red pepper	1 cup	250 mL
Frozen concentrated apple juice, thawed	2 tbsp.	30 mL
Liquid honey	2 tbsp.	30 mL
Rice vinegar	2 tbsp.	30 mL
Sesame oil (for flavour)	1 tsp.	5 mL
Soy sauce	1 tsp.	5 mL
Ground ginger	1/2 tsp.	2 mL
Garlic powder	1/4 tsp.	1 mL
Pepper	1/4 tsp.	1 mL

Combine first 3 ingredients in medium bowl.

Whisk remaining 8 ingredients in small bowl. Drizzle over suey choy mixture. Toss. Chill, covered, for 30 minutes to blend flavours. Makes about 6 cups (1.5 L).

1 cup (250 mL): 62 Calories; 1.0 g Total Fat (0.3 g Mono, 0.4 g Poly, 0.2 g Sat); 0 mg Cholesterol; 13 g Carbohydrate; 2 g Fibre; 1 g Protein; 91 mg Sodium

Autumn Squash Bake

Looking for something light and fluffy to go with turkey or ham?
This citrus-spiced bake has all the light texture of a soufflé,
with none of the work. Use any orange-fleshed squash
or even canned pure pumpkin if you're in a pinch.

Mashed cooked squash	4 cups	1 L
(about 3 lbs, 1.4 kg, uncooked)		
Milk	1 cup	250 mL
Fine dry bread crumbs	1/2 cup	125 mL
Butter (or hard margarine), melted	2 tbsp.	30 mL
Ground cinnamon	1/4 tsp.	1 mL
Salt	1/2 tsp.	2 mL
Pepper	1/4 tsp	1 mL
Ground cardamom	1/8 tsp.	0.5 mL
Ground nutmeg, just a pinch		
Large eggs, fork-beaten	3	3
Frozen concentrated orange juice, thawed	2 tbsp.	30 mL
Fine dry bread crumbs	3 tbsp.	50 mL
Butter (or hard margarine), melted	1 tbsp.	15 mL

Combine first 9 ingredients in large bowl. Let stand for 5 minutes.

Add eggs and concentrated orange juice. Stir. Spread evenly in greased 2 quart (2 L) casserole.

Combine second amounts of bread crumbs and melted butter in small bowl. Sprinkle over squash mixture. Bake, covered, in 350°F (175°C) oven for about 70 minutes until wooden pick inserted in centre comes out clean. Cuts into 8 pieces.

1 piece: 164 Calories; 7.0 g Total Fat (2.3 g Mono, 0.6 g Poly, 3.6 g Sat); 83 mg Cholesterol; 21 g Carbohydrate; 3 g Fibre; 6 g Protein; 299 mg Sodium

Variation: For a sweeter version, drizzle with maple syrup or sprinkle with brown sugar before baking.

Golden Fried Plantains

Not all tropical island treasures are made up of gold and jewels! Crispy golden "coins" of fried plantain are a valuable addition to a meal of Caribbean dishes.

All-purpose flour	1/4 cup	60 mL
Cayenne pepper	1 1/2 tsp.	7 mL
Salt	1/2 tsp.	2 mL
Paprika, sprinkle		
Ripe plantains (see Note)	2	2
Cooking oil, approximately	1 1/2 cups	375 mL

Combine first 4 ingredients in medium resealable freezer bag.

Cut and discard ends of plantains. Slit peel lengthwise along inside curve, being careful not to cut into flesh. Remove and discard peel. Cut plantains into thin slices, about 1/8 inch (3 mm) thick. Add to flour mixture. Seal bag. Toss until coated. Remove to plate. Discard any remaining flour mixture.

Pour cooking oil into large saucepan until about 1/2 inch (12 mm) deep. Heat on medium-high until hot. Cook plantain in 4 batches, for about 5 minutes per batch, turning at halftime, until golden. Transfer with slotted spoon to paper towel-lined plate to drain. Makes about 2 cups (500 mL).

1 cup (250 mL): 500 Calories; 28.1 g Total Fat (16.1 g Mono, 8.3 g Poly, 2.2 g Sat); 0 mg Cholesterol; 66 g Carbohydrate; 5 g Fibre; 4 g Protein; 446 mg Sodium

Note: Green plantains are unripe; light yellow plantains with few or no black spots are semi-ripe; black plantains are ripe. Grocery stores usually carry unripened plantains. To ripen, store in brown paper bag at room temperature. It usually takes 7 to 8 days to fully ripen.

Summer Salad

This crisp and fruity summer side is also a certified cure for the winter blues!
Substitute Balkan yogurt for richer flavour and texture.

Thinly sliced English cucumber (with peel)	1 cup	250 mL
Thinly sliced radish	1 cup	250 mL
Thinly sliced tart apple (such as Granny Smith)	1 cup	250 mL
Plain yogurt	1/2 cup	125 mL
Lemon juice	3 tbsp.	50 mL
Finely chopped fresh dill (or 1 1/2 tsp., 7 mL, dried)	2 tbsp.	30 mL
Liquid honey	1 tbsp.	15 mL
Salt	1/2 tsp.	2 mL
Pepper, just a pinch		

Combine first 3 ingredients in medium bowl.

Whisk remaining 6 ingredients in small bowl until smooth. Add to cucumber mixture. Toss until coated. Makes about 3 cups (750 mL).

1 cup (250 mL): 114 Calories; 2.5 g Total Fat (0.7 g Mono, 0.1 g Poly, 1.6 g Sat); 7 mg Cholesterol; 22 g Carbohydrate; 2 g Fibre; 2 g Protein; 430 mg Sodium

Tangy Carrots

The sweet, spicy and tangy flavours will show you how versatile carrots can be.

Bag of baby carrots, larger ones cut in half lengthwise	1 lb.	454 g
Thinly sliced yellow pepper	1 cup	250 mL
Finely chopped onion	1/4 cup	60 mL
Cooking oil	3 tbsp.	50 mL
Liquid honey	2 tbsp.	30 mL
White vinegar	2 tbsp.	30 mL
Dijon mustard	2 tsp.	10 mL
Salt	1/8 tsp.	0.5 mL
Pepper	1/8 tsp.	0.5 mL

(continued on next page)

Pour water into medium saucepan until about 1 inch (2.5 cm) deep. Add carrots. Bring to a boil. Reduce heat to medium. Boil, uncovered, for 8 to 10 minutes until tender-crisp. Drain. Transfer to medium bowl. Add yellow pepper.

Whisk remaining 7 ingredients in small bowl. Drizzle over carrot mixture. Toss. Makes about 3 cups (750 mL).

1 cup (250 mL): 242 Calories; 14.5 g Total Fat (8.1 g Mono, 4.5 g Poly, 1.1 g Sat); 0 mg Cholesterol; 28 g Carbohydrate; 3 g Fibre; 2 g Protein; 195 mg Sodium

Pictured on front cover.

Cabbage And Apples

You're cooking a meal of sausage, ham or chicken—but something's missing. You need something a little bit sweet, yet a little bit tart to balance out the meat's richness. May we suggest this tender-crisp blend of cabbage and apple?

Olive (or cooking) oil	1 tbsp.	15 mL
Chopped onion	1 cup	250 mL
Shredded green cabbage, lightly packed	4 cups	1 L
Caraway seed	1/2 tsp.	1 mL
Chopped unpeeled tart apple (such as Granny Smith)	2 cups	500 mL
White wine vinegar	3 tbsp.	50 mL
Granulated sugar	1 1/2 tsp.	7 mL
Salt	1/4 tsp.	1 mL
Pepper	1/4 tsp.	1 mL

Heat olive oil in large frying pan on medium. Add onion. Cook for 5 to 10 minutes, stirring occasionally, until softened.

Add cabbage and caraway seed. Stir. Cook, partially covered, for 3 to 5 minutes, stirring occasionally, until tender-crisp.

Add remaining 5 ingredients. Heat and stir for about 2 minutes until heated through. Makes about 3 cups (750 mL).

1 cup (250 mL): 137 Calories; 4.9 g Total Fat (3.4 g Mono, 0.5 g Poly, 0.7 g Sat); 0 mg Cholesterol; 24 g Carbohydrate; 5 g Fibre; 2 g Protein; 214 mg Sodium

Basil Feta Spaghetti Squash

Soft strands of spaghetti squash are tossed with flavourful garlic, feta and basil in this versatile microwave dish. Serve with chicken, pork or fish.

Spaghetti squash	3 1/2 lbs.	1.6 kg
Water	2 tbsp.	30 mL
Pine nuts	1/3 cup	75 mL
Olive oil	1 tbsp.	15 mL
Garlic clove, minced	1	1
(or 1/4 tsp., 1 mL, powder)		
Crumbled feta cheese	1/2 cup	125 mL
Chopped fresh basil	2 tbsp.	30 mL
Butter (or hard margarine)	1 tbsp.	15 mL
Salt	1/2 tsp.	2 mL
Pepper	1/4 tsp.	1 mL

Cut squash in half lengthwise. Remove seeds. Place, cut-side down, in large ungreased microwave-safe 2 quart (2 L) casserole. Add water. Microwave, covered, on high (100%) for about 15 minutes until tender. Drain. Shred squash pulp with fork. Separate into strands. Transfer to large bowl. Cover to keep warm. Discard shells.

Combine pine nuts and olive oil in small microwave-safe bowl. Microwave, uncovered, on high (100%) for about 2 minutes, stirring twice, until golden and toasted.

Add garlic. Stir. Microwave on high (100%) for about 1 minute until garlic is softened. Add to squash.

Add remaining 5 ingredients. Stir until cheese starts to soften. Makes about 3 1/4 cups (800 mL).

1 cup (250 mL): 377 Calories; 23.8 g Total Fat (8.4 g Mono, 5.3 g Poly, 8.2 g Sat); 30 mg Cholesterol; 38 g Carbohydrate; 8 g Fibre; 11 g Protein; 735 mg Sodium

Blender Hollandaise Sauce

If you think Hollandaise sauce has to be fiddly, you won't believe
how easy and speedy it is when you make it in your blender!
Serve on asparagus, fish or poached eggs.

Large eggs (see Note)	2	2
Lemon juice	1 tbsp.	15 mL
White wine vinegar	1 tbsp.	15 mL
Cayenne pepper, sprinkle		
Salt, sprinkle		
Pepper, sprinkle		
Butter (or hard margarine)	1 cup	250 mL

Put first 6 ingredients into blender. Process until smooth.

Put butter into small microwave-safe bowl. Microwave, uncovered, on high (100%) for 1 1/2 to 2 minutes until melted and bubbling. With motor running, add butter in thin stream through hole in lid until sauce is thickened. Makes about 1 3/4 cups (425 mL).

2 tbsp. (30 mL): 125 Calories; 13.7 g Total Fat (3.7 g Mono, 0.6 g Poly, 8.4 g Sat);
61 mg Cholesterol; trace Carbohydrate; 0 g Fibre; 101 g Protein; 101 mg Sodium

Note: This recipe uses raw eggs. Make sure to use fresh, clean Grade A eggs. Keep chilled and consume the same day it is prepared. Always discard leftovers. Pregnant women, young children or the elderly are not advised to eat anything containing raw egg.

Greek Tomato Sauce

Looking for a tip-top topper for chicken, fish or pasta? Look no further than this chunky tomato sauce with the tangy taste of lemon and olives.

Cooking oil	2 tsp.	10 mL
Chopped onion	1 cup	250 mL
Garlic cloves, minced	2	2
(or 1/2 tsp., 2 mL, powder)		
All-purpose flour	1 tbsp.	15 mL
Prepared chicken (or vegetable) broth	1/2 cup	125 mL
Can of diced tomatoes (with juice)	14 oz.	398 mL
Grated lemon zest	1 tbsp.	15 mL
Dried oregano	1/2 tsp.	2 mL
Ground cumin	1/2 tsp.	2 mL
Pepper	1/8 tsp.	0.5 mL
Sliced black olives (optional)	1/2 cup	125 mL

Heat cooking oil in large frying pan on medium. Add onion and garlic. Cook for 5 to 10 minutes, stirring occasionally, until onion is softened.

Add flour. Heat and stir for 1 minute. Slowly add broth, stirring constantly, until smooth. Heat and stir until boiling and thickened. Add next 5 ingredients. Stir. Cook, covered, for 5 minutes, stirring occasionally, to blend flavours.

Add olives. Stir. Makes about 2 cups (500 mL).

1/4 cup (60 mL): 34 Calories; 1.3 g Total Fat (0.7 g Mono, 0.4 g Poly, 0.1 g Sat); 0 mg Cholesterol; 5 g Carbohydrate; trace Fibre; 1 g Protein; 229 mg Sodium

Peach Lime Chutney

This spicy chutney will knock your socks off! The combination of ginger, lime and peach pairs perfectly with grilled chicken, pork chops or baked ham.

Can of sliced peaches in light syrup, drained and chopped	28 oz.	796 mL
Granulated sugar	2/3 cup	150 mL
Apple cider vinegar	1/2 cup	125 mL
Chopped dried apricot	1/2 cup	125 mL
Chopped onion	1/2 cup	125 mL
Minced crystallized ginger	2 tbsp.	30 mL
Lime juice	1 tbsp.	15 mL
Grated lime zest	2 tsp.	10 mL
Dried crushed chilies	1/4 tsp.	1 mL
Ground allspice	1/4 tsp.	1 mL
Salt	1/4 tsp.	1 mL
Pepper	1/4 tsp.	1 mL

Combine all 12 ingredients in large saucepan. Bring to a boil. Reduce heat to medium-low. Simmer, uncovered, for about 30 minutes, stirring occasionally, until thickened. Store in airtight container in refrigerator for up to 2 weeks. Makes about 3 cups (750 mL).

2 tbsp. (30 mL): 57 Calories; 0.1 g Total Fat (trace Mono, trace Poly, 0 g Sat); 0 mg Cholesterol; 15 g Carbohydrate; 1 g Fibre; trace Protein; 28 mg Sodium

Pictured on page 143.

Paré Pointer

The best way to make an egg roll is to push it.

Spicy Mustard

Specialty home-made mustards are all the rage these days.
Join the in-crowd and try this spicy condiment that's superb with
grilled steak, baked ham, pork chops, burgers and hot dogs.

Mustard seed	1/3 cup	75 mL
Dry (or alcohol-free) white wine	1/4 cup	60 mL
Water	1/4 cup	60 mL
White wine vinegar	1/4 cup	60 mL
Liquid honey	2 tbsp.	30 mL
Prepared horseradish	2 tsp.	10 mL
Coarse salt	1/4 tsp.	1 mL
Ground allspice	1/4 tsp.	1 mL
Turmeric	1/4 tsp.	1 mL

Combine first 4 ingredients in small bowl. Let stand, covered, for at least 8 hours or overnight. Transfer to blender or food processor.

Add remaining 5 ingredients. Process until thick and almost smooth. Store in airtight container in refrigerator for up to 3 weeks. Makes about 1 cup (250 mL).

1 tbsp. (15 mL): 26 Calories; 0.9 g Total Fat (0.6 g Mono, 0.2 g Poly, 0.1 g Sat); 0 mg Cholesterol; 3 g Carbohydrate; 1 g Fibre; 1 g Protein; 31 mg Sodium

Ginger Cranberry Sauce

Typical cranberry sauce is given extra oomph with the added flavours
of ginger and orange. Serve with roast turkey or baked ham.

Bag of frozen (or fresh) cranberries	12 oz.	340 g
Granulated sugar	3/4 cup	175 mL
Orange juice	2/3 cup	150 mL
Water	1/4 cup	60 mL
Grated orange zest	1 1/2 tsp.	7 mL
Ground ginger	1/2 tsp.	2 mL
Minced crystallized ginger	1/4 cup	60 mL

(continued on next page)

Combine first 6 ingredients in medium saucepan. Bring to a boil. Reduce heat to medium. Stir until sugar is dissolved. Boil gently for about 5 minutes, stirring occasionally, until cranberries split. Remove from heat.

Stir in crystallized ginger. Store in airtight container in refrigerator for up to 2 weeks. Makes about 2 2/3 cups (650 mL).

2 tbsp. (30 mL): 47 Calories; 0.1 g Total Fat (0 g Mono, trace Poly, 0 g Sat); 0 mg Cholesterol; 12 g Carbohydrate; 1 g Fibre; trace Protein; 2 mg Sodium

Pictured on page 143.

Chimichurri

Chimichurri (pronounced chim-ME-chur-EE) is a traditional savoury Argentinean condiment that is most commonly served with beef but also works well as a dip. You'll love it with chicken or pork too!

Fresh parsley, lightly packed	2 cups	500 mL
Chopped fresh oregano	2 tbsp.	30 mL
Chopped red onion	2 tbsp.	30 mL
White wine vinegar	1 1/2 tbsp.	25 mL
Garlic cloves	2	2
Dried crushed chilies	1/2 tsp.	2 mL
Salt	1/2 tsp.	2 mL
Pepper	1/2 tsp.	2 mL
Olive oil	1/4 cup	60 mL

Put first 8 ingredients into blender or food processor. Pulse with on/off motion until coarse paste forms.

With motor running, add olive oil in thin stream through hole in lid or feed chute until smooth. Transfer to small bowl. Chill, covered, for 2 hours to blend flavours. Store in airtight container in refrigerator for up to 1 week. Serve at room temperature. Makes about 2/3 cup (150 mL).

1 tbsp. (15 mL): 55 Calories; 5.5 g Total Fat (4.0 g Mono, 0.5 g Poly, 0.8 g Sat); 0 mg Cholesterol; 1 g Carbohydrate; trace Fibre; trace Protein; 124 mg Sodium

Pictured on page 143.

Golden Cucumber Pickles

Think only Grandma could have enough patience to make pickles from scratch? These easy cukes are ready in hours, not days, and add a pretty golden colour to any plate.

English cucumbers, peeled, halved lengthwise, seeds removed and cut into 1/4 inch (6 mm) slices	2	2
Diced onion	1/2 cup	125 mL
Olive oil	1/2 cup	125 mL
White vinegar	1/3 cup	75 mL
Granulated sugar	2 tbsp.	30 mL
Dried dillweed	1 tsp.	5 mL
Turmeric	1 tsp.	5 mL
Salt	1 tsp.	5 mL
Pepper	1/4 tsp.	1 mL
Chopped fresh parsley	1 tbsp.	15 mL

Put cucumber and onion into large bowl.

Whisk next 7 ingredients in small bowl. Add to cucumber mixture. Toss. Chill, covered, for 2 hours, tossing occasionally. Transfer to serving bowl, using slotted spoon. Drizzle 1/3 cup (75 mL) olive oil mixture over cucumber. Discard remaining olive oil mixture.

Sprinkle with parsley. Makes about 3 cups (750 mL).

1/4 cup (60 mL): 29 Calories; 2.3 g Total Fat (1.6 g Mono, 0.2 g Poly, 0.3 g Sat); 0 mg Cholesterol; 2 g Carbohydrate; trace Fibre; trace Protein; 48 mg Sodium

Pictured at right.

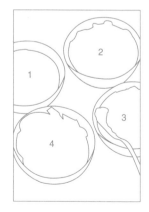

1. Ginger Cranberry Sauce, page 140
2. Peach Lime Chutney, page 139
3. Chimichurri, page 141
4. Golden Cucumber Pickles, above

Props courtesy of: Stokes

Speedy Applesauce

From apples to sauce in only 15 minutes! Try it with your
favourite variety of apple, or increase the honey if you've
got a sweet tooth. Great with ham or pork.

Chopped peeled cooking apple (such as McIntosh)	3 cups	750 mL
Chopped peeled tart apple (such as Granny Smith)	3 cups	750 mL
Apple juice	1/4 cup	60 mL
Liquid honey	1 tbsp.	15 mL
Ground cinnamon	1/2 tsp.	2 mL

Combine first 3 ingredients in medium microwave-safe bowl. Microwave, covered, on high (100%) for about 10 minutes until apple is softened. Mash until almost smooth.

Add honey and cinnamon. Stir. Store in airtight container in refrigerator for up to 1 week. Makes about 3 cups (750 mL).

1/4 cup (60 mL): 39 Calories; 0.1 g Total Fat (0 g Mono, trace Poly, trace Sat); 0 mg Cholesterol; 10 g Carbohydrate; 2 g Fibre; trace Protein; 1 mg Sodium

NUTTY APPLESAUCE: Stir in 1 cup (250 mL) chopped toasted walnuts with honey and cinnamon.

1. Hearty Rice Salad, page 97
2. Roasted Fennel Ratatouille, page 101

Props courtesy of: Danesco Inc.
Stokes

Mustard Sauce

This très chic *sauce has hints of wine, lemon and Dijon—and is sure to add elegance to a main course of chicken or fish.*

Butter (or hard margarine)	2 tsp.	10 mL
Finely chopped onion	1/3 cup	75 mL
Garlic cloves, minced	2	2
(or 1/2 tsp., 2 mL, powder)		
Dry (or alcohol-free) white wine	1/2 cup	125 mL
Prepared chicken broth	1 1/2 cups	375 mL
Dijon mustard	3 tbsp.	50 mL
Lemon juice	1 tbsp.	15 mL
Salt	1/4 tsp.	1 mL
Pepper	1/4 tsp.	1 mL
Prepared chicken broth	2 tbsp.	30 mL
Cornstarch	1 tbsp.	15 mL
Half-and-half cream	1/4 cup	60 mL
Chopped fresh parsley	2 tbsp.	30 mL

Melt butter in small saucepan on medium. Add onion and garlic. Cook for about 5 minutes, stirring often, until onion is softened.

Add wine. Heat and stir for 2 minutes. Add next 5 ingredients. Stir. Bring to a boil. Reduce heat to medium-low. Simmer, uncovered, for 5 minutes to blend flavours.

Stir second amount of broth into cornstarch in small cup. Add to mustard mixture. Heat and stir for 1 to 2 minutes until boiling and thickened. Remove from heat.

Stir in cream and parsley. Makes about 2 cups (500 mL).

2 tbsp. (30 mL): 20 Calories; 1.0 g Total Fat (0.3 g Mono, 0.1 g Poly, 0.6 g Sat); 3 mg Cholesterol; 1 g Carbohydrate; trace Fibre; trace Protein; 217 mg Sodium

Creamy Mushroom Sauce

*With the richness of brandy and cream, this sauce is sure to elevate
even the most humble of roast meat dinners. If serving with beef or lamb,
use beef broth. If serving with poultry or pork, use chicken broth.*

Butter	1/4 cup	60 mL
Finely chopped onion	1/2 cup	125 mL
Garlic clove, minced	1	1
(or 1/4 tsp., 1 mL, powder)		
Sliced fresh white mushrooms	4 cups	1 L
All-purpose flour	1/4 cup	60 mL
Prepared chicken (or beef) broth	1 1/2 cups	375 mL
Brandy	2 tbsp.	30 mL
Half-and-half cream	1/4 cup	60 mL
Salt	1/4 tsp.	1 mL
Pepper	1/4 tsp.	1 mL

Melt butter in large frying pan on medium. Add onion and garlic. Cook for about 5 minutes, stirring occasionally, until onion is softened.

Add mushrooms. Cook for about 10 minutes, stirring occasionally, until mushrooms start to brown and liquid is evaporated.

Add flour. Heat and stir for 1 minute. Slowly add broth, stirring constantly, until smooth. Add brandy. Heat and stir for 2 to 4 minutes until boiling and thickened.

Add remaining 3 ingredients. Stir. Makes about 3 1/4 cups (800 mL).

1/4 cup (60 mL): 59 Calories; 4.1 g Total Fat (1.1 g Mono, 0.2 g Poly, 2.5 g Sat); 11 mg Cholesterol; 3 g Carbohydrate; trace Fibre; 1 g Protein; 238 mg Sodium

Paré Pointer

The city kid thought the best way to raise potatoes was on a fork.

Cabbage Relish

You'll relish the thought of your next dinner of grilled chicken, pork, lamb or sausages when it's accompanied by this colourful and tangy condiment. Can be served chilled or at room temperature.

Finely chopped red cabbage, lightly packed	2 cups	500 mL
Finely chopped onion	1 cup	250 mL
Granulated sugar	1/3 cup	75 mL
Red wine vinegar	1/3 cup	75 mL
Water	1/4 cup	60 mL
Celery seed	1 tsp.	5 mL
Mustard seed	1 tsp.	5 mL
Dried crushed chilies	1/2 tsp.	2 mL
Ground cinnamon	1/2 tsp.	2 mL
Salt	1 tsp.	5 mL

Combine all 10 ingredients in medium saucepan. Bring to a boil. Reduce heat to medium. Cook, uncovered, for about 25 minutes, stirring occasionally, until cabbage is tender. Store in airtight container in refrigerator for up to 2 weeks. Makes about 1 1/2 cups (375 mL).

2 tbsp. (30 mL): 30 Calories; 0.2 g Total Fat (0.1 g Mono, trace Poly, trace Sat); 0 mg Cholesterol; 7 g Carbohydrate; 1 g Fibre; trace Protein; 190 mg Sodium

Sweet And Sour Sauce

Our version of this traditional salty, sweet and tart sauce has plenty of fresh fruit flavour. Excellent with chicken or pork.

Cooking oil	1 tsp.	5 mL
Chopped onion	1 cup	250 mL
Can of crushed pineapple, drained	14 oz.	398 mL
Apricot jam, larger pieces chopped	1 cup	250 mL
Soy sauce	1 tbsp.	15 mL
White vinegar	1 tbsp.	15 mL

Heat cooking oil in medium saucepan on medium. Add onion. Cook for 5 to 10 minutes, stirring often, until softened.

(continued on next page)

Add remaining 4 ingredients. Cook and stir until heated through. Store in airtight container in refrigerator for up to 1 week. Makes about 2 1/3 cups (575 mL).

2 tbsp. (30 mL): 59 Calories; 0.3 g Total Fat (0.2 g Mono, 0.1 g Poly, trace Sat); 0 mg Cholesterol; 15 g Carbohydrate; trace Fibre; trace Protein; 48 mg Sodium

Chipotle Red Pepper Ketchup

Customize your basic burgers, hot dogs and fries
with this sweet and smoky ketchup.

Can of tomato sauce	14 oz.	398 mL
Chopped onion	1 cup	250 mL
Chopped roasted red peppers	1 cup	250 mL
Brown sugar, packed	1/3 cup	75 mL
Apple cider vinegar	1/4 cup	60 mL
Finely chopped chipotle pepper in adobo sauce (see Tip, page 49)	1 1/2 tsp.	7 mL
Cooking oil	1 tsp.	5 mL
Ground cumin	1/4 tsp.	1 mL
Salt	1/4 tsp.	1 mL
Pepper	1/4 tsp.	1 mL

Combine all 10 ingredients in small saucepan. Bring to a boil. Reduce heat to medium-low. Simmer, uncovered, for 10 minutes, stirring often to blend flavours. Carefully process with hand blender or in blender until smooth. Store in airtight container in refrigerator for up to 2 weeks. Makes about 3 1/3 cups (825 mL).

1 tbsp. (15 mL): 15 Calories; 0.1 g Total Fat (0.1 g Mono, trace Poly, trace Sat); 0 mg Cholesterol; 3 g Carbohydrate; trace Fibre; trace Protein; 99 mg Sodium

Measurement Tables

Throughout this book measurements are given in Conventional and Metric measure. To compensate for differences between the two measurements due to rounding, a full metric measure is not always used. The cup used is the standard 8 fluid ounce. Temperature is given in degrees Fahrenheit and Celsius. Baking pan measurements are in inches and centimetres as well as quarts and litres. An exact metric conversion is given below as well as the working equivalent (Metric Standard Measure).

Spoons

Conventional Measure	Metric Exact Conversion Millilitre (mL)	Metric Standard Measure Millilitre (mL)
1/8 teaspoon (tsp.)	0.6 mL	0.5 mL
1/4 teaspoon (tsp.)	1.2 mL	1 mL
1/2 teaspoon (tsp.)	2.4 mL	2 mL
1 teaspoon (tsp.)	4.7 mL	5 mL
2 teaspoons (tsp.)	9.4 mL	10 mL
1 tablespoon (tbsp.)	14.2 mL	15 mL

Cups

Conventional Measure	Metric Exact Conversion Millilitre (mL)	Metric Standard Measure Millilitre (mL)
1/4 cup (4 tbsp.)	56.8 mL	60 mL
1/3 cup (5 1/3 tbsp.)	75.6 mL	75 mL
1/2 cup (8 tbsp.)	113.7 mL	125 mL
2/3 cup (10 2/3 tbsp.)	151.2 mL	150 mL
3/4 cup (12 tbsp.)	170.5 mL	175 mL
1 cup (16 tbsp.)	227.3 mL	250 mL
4 1/2 cups	1022.9 mL	1000 mL (1 L)

Oven Temperatures

Fahrenheit (°F)	Celsius (°C)
175°	80°
200°	95°
225°	110°
250°	120°
275°	140°
300°	150°
325°	160°
350°	175°
375°	190°
400°	205°
425°	220°
450°	230°
475°	240°
500°	260°

Dry Measurements

Conventional Measure Ounces (oz.)	Metric Exact Conversion Grams (g)	Metric Standard Measure Grams (g)
1 oz.	28.3 g	28 g
2 oz.	56.7 g	57 g
3 oz.	85.0 g	85 g
4 oz.	113.4 g	125 g
5 oz.	141.7 g	140 g
6 oz.	170.1 g	170 g
7 oz.	198.4 g	200 g
8 oz.	226.8 g	250 g
16 oz.	453.6 g	500 g
32 oz.	907.2 g	1000 g (1 kg)

Pans

Conventional Inches	Metric Centimetres
8x8 inch	20x20 cm
9x9 inch	22x22 cm
9x13 inch	22x33 cm
10x15 inch	25x38 cm
11x17 inch	28x43 cm
8x2 inch round	20x5 cm
9x2 inch round	22x5 cm
10x4 1/2 inch tube	25x11 cm
8x4x3 inch loaf	20x10x7.5 cm
9x5x3 inch loaf	22x12.5x7.5 cm

Casseroles

CANADA & BRITAIN		UNITED STATES	
Standard Size Casserole	Exact Metric Measure	Standard Size Casserole	Exact Metric Measure
1 qt. (5 cups)	1.13 L	1 qt. (4 cups)	900 mL
1 1/2 qts. (7 1/2 cups)	1.69 L	1 1/2 qts. (6 cups)	1.35 L
2 qts. (10 cups)	2.25 L	2 qts. (8 cups)	1.8 L
2 1/2 qts. (12 1/2 cups)	2.81 L	2 1/2 qts. (10 cups)	2.25 L
3 qts. (15 cups)	3.38 L	3 qts. (12 cups)	2.7 L
4 qts. (20 cups)	4.5 L	4 qts. (16 cups)	3.6 L
5 qts. (25 cups)	5.63 L	5 qts. (20 cups)	4.5 L

Recipe Index

Company's Coming cookbooks are available at retail locations throughout Canada!

EXCLUSIVE mail order offer on next page

Buy any 2 cookbooks—choose a 3rd FREE of equal or lesser value than the lowest price paid.

Original Series — $15.99

CODE		CODE		CODE	
SQ	150 Delicious Squares	PB	The Potato Book	WM	30-Minute Weekday Meals
CA	Casseroles	CCLFC	Low-Fat Cooking	SDL	School Days Lunches
MU	Muffins & More	SCH	Stews, Chilies & Chowders	PD	Potluck Dishes
SA	Salads	FD	Fondues	GBR	Ground Beef Recipes
AP	Appetizers	CCBE	The Beef Book	FRIR	4-Ingredient Recipes
CO	Cookies	RC	The Rookie Cook	KHC	Kids' Healthy Cooking
PA	Pasta	RHR	Rush-Hour Recipes	MM	Mostly Muffins
BA	Barbecues	SW	Sweet Cravings	SP	Soups
PR	Preserves	YRG	Year-Round Grilling	SU	Simple Suppers
CH	Chicken, Etc.	GG	Garden Greens	CCDC	Diabetic Cooking
CT	Cooking For Two	CHC	Chinese Cooking	CHN	Chicken Now
SC	Slow Cooker Recipes	RL	Recipes For Leftovers	KDS	Kids Do Snacks
SF	Stir-Fry	BEV	The Beverage Book	TMRC	30-Minute Rookie Cook
MAM	Make-Ahead Meals	SCD	Slow Cooker Dinners	LFE	Low-Fat Express

Cookbook Author Biography

CODE	$15.99
JP	Jean Paré: An Appetite for Life

Most Loved Recipe Collection

CODE	$23.99
MLBQ	Most Loved Barbecuing
MLCO	Most Loved Cookies

CODE	$24.99
MLSD	Most Loved Salads & Dressings
MLCA	Most Loved Casseroles
MLSF	Most Loved Stir-Fries
MLHF	Most Loved Holiday Favourites
MLSC	Most Loved Slow Cooker Creationss
MLDE	Most Loved Summertime Desserts

3-in-1 Cookbook Collection

CODE	$29.99
MNT	Meals in No Time
MME	Meals Made Easy NEW June 1/08

Lifestyle Series

CODE	$17.99
DC	Diabetic Cooking

CODE	$19.99
DDI	Diabetic Dinners
HR	Easy Healthy Recipes
HH	Healthy in a Hurry
WGR	Whole Grain Recipes

Special Occasion Series

CODE	$20.99
GFK	Gifts from the Kitchen

CODE	$24.99
MLBQ	Christmas Gifts from the Kitchen
TR	Timeless Recipes for All Occasions

CODE	$27.99
CCEL	Christmas Celebrations

CODE	$29.99
CATH	Cooking At Home

Order **ONLINE** for fast delivery!

Log onto **www.companyscoming.com**, browse through our library of cookbooks, gift sets and newest releases and place your order using our fast and secure online order form.

Title	Code	Quantity	Price	Total
			$	$

TOTAL BOOKS (including FREE)		TOTAL BOOKS PURCHASED:	

	International	USA	Canada
Shipping & Handling First Book (per destination)	$ 11.98 (one book)	$ 6.98 (one book)	$ 5.98 (one book)
Additional Books (include FREE books)	$ ($4.99 each)	$ ($1.99 each)	$ ($1.99 each)
Sub-Total	$	$	$
Canadian residents add GST/HST			$
TOTAL AMOUNT ENCLOSED	$	$	$

Terms
- All orders must be prepaid. Sorry, no CODs.
- Prices are listed in Canadian Funds for Canadian orders, or US funds for US & International orders.
- Prices are subject to change without prior notice.
- Canadian residents must pay GST/HST (no provincial tax required).
- No tax is required for orders outside Canada.
- Satisfaction is guaranteed or return within 30 days for a full refund.
- Make cheque or money order payable to: **Company's Coming Publishing Limited** 2311-96 Street, Edmonton, Alberta Canada T6N 1G3.
- Orders are shipped surface mail. For courier rates, visit our website: **www.companyscoming.com** or contact us: **Tel: 780-450-6223 Fax: 780-450-1857.**

Gift Giving
- Let us help you with your gift giving!
- We will send cookbooks directly to the recipients of your choice if you give us their names and addresses.
- Please specify the titles you wish to send to each person.
- If you would like to include a personal note or card, we will be pleased to enclose it with your gift order.
- Company's Coming Cookbooks make excellent gifts: birthdays, bridal showers, Mother's Day, Father's Day, graduation or any occasion …collect them all!

☐ MasterCard ☐ VISA Expiry ____/____ MO/YR

Credit Card # _____

Name of cardholder _____

Cardholder signature _____

Shipping Address Send the cookbooks listed above to:
☐ **Please check if this is a Gift Order**

Name: _____

Street: _____

City: _____ Prov./State: _____

Postal Code/Zip: _____ Country: _____

Tel: ( ) _____

E-mail address: _____

Your privacy is important to us. We will not share your e-mail address or personal information with any outside party.

☐ **YES! Please add me to your News Bite e-mail newsletter.**

Cookmark

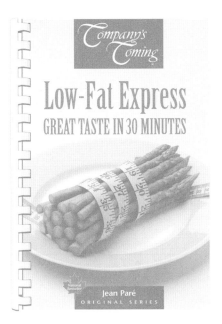

Healthy fast food for the whole family is easy with *Low-Fat Express*! Ready in less than 30 minutes from start to finish, these great-tasting recipes dish up under 10 g of fat per serving. Guilt-free breakfasts, suppers, snacks and desserts— in a flash!

COOKBOOKS

Quick
&
Easy
Recipes

Everyday
Ingredients

Canada's
most popular
cookbooks!